JOHANNES TAUTZ—author, historian, religious scholar, anthroposophist and Waldorf teacher (at the first Steiner school in Stuttgart, Germany)— was born in 1914 in Koblenz. He studied German and History, graduating with a dissertation on Schelling. The author of *W.J. Stein, A Biography*, he lives in Darmstadt, Germany.

ATTACK OF THE ENEMY

The Occult Inspiration Behind Adolf Hitler and the Nazis

An Esoteric Study

Johannes Tautz

TEMPLE LODGE

First published in Great Britain in 2014 by
Temple Lodge Publishing,
Hillside House, The Square
Forest Row, RH18 5ES

E-mail: office@templelodge.com

www.templelodge.com

Originally published in German under the title *Der Eingriff des Widersachers – Fragen zum okkulten Aspekt des Nationalsozialismus* by Verlag Die Kommenden, Freiburg i.B. 1976. New edition with additional material by Perseus Verlag, Basel, 2002

Appendix by Andreas Bracher first published as 'Der Völkishe Beobachter und Rudolf Steiner – Materialien zur Erhellung des Gegensatz-verhältnisses von Nazibewegung und Anthroposophie nach dem Ersten Weltkrieg' in *Der Europäer*, Year 5, No. 2/3 (Dec. 2000/Jan. 2001)

Appendix and Bibliography translated by Johanna Collis

A catalogue record for this book is available from the British Library

ISBN 978 1 906999 71 1

Cover by Morgan Creative
Typeset by DP Photosetting, Neath, West Glamorgan
Printed and bound by 4edge Limited, Essex, UK

Contents

Publisher's Note

As the author describes in his Preface, this booklet is essentially a transcript of lectures presented to members of the Anthroposophical Society in 1966 (33 years after the Nazis first assumed power in 1933). First published in 1976, it should be seen as something of an historical piece. Yet it remains one of the most significant attempts to form a spiritual understanding of the phenomenon of National Socialism.

Tautz's perspective is informed by his study of the philosophy developed by Rudolf Steiner (1861–1925), known as anthroposophy or spiritual science. Although some additional notes have been added to the text, the author assumes a basic understanding of Steiner's terminology and worldview.

This first English edition features the entire text by Tautz, but also additional material compiled and edited by Andreas Bracher for the new edition published by Perseus Verlag in 2002. This material includes a review of important texts on Nazism published in recent decades, as well as excerpts from the Nazi 'house magazine', *Völkische Beobachter*, demonstrating the vicious attacks and hatred directed at Rudolf Steiner and the anthroposophical movement by the National Socialists. (The first extract — from 1921 — is even penned by Adolf Hitler himself.) In the light of contemporary attacks against the anthroposophical movement and Rudolf Steiner schools, with attempts being made to somehow link anthroposophy with Nazi ideology, this material is particularly valuable and revealing.

Tautz refers to Hermann Rauschning and his book *Hitler Speaks*, which is supposedly based on conversations with Adolf Hitler between 1932 and 1934. Rauschning was a former Nazi who renounced his party membership and emigrated from Germany in 1936, eventually settling in the United States. In 1976, when this book was first published in German, Rauschning's work was widely regarded as authentic by historians of the stature of Hugh Trevor-Roper. More recently, however, the veracity of the content of his book has been questioned and discredited, principally by Swiss researcher Wolfgang Hänel. However, in 2000 Hugh Trevor-Roper wrote: 'Rauschning may have yielded at times to journalistic temptations, but he had opportunities to record Hitler's conversations and the general tenor of his record too exactly foretells Hitler's later utterances to be dismissed as fabrication.'[*]

The present translation of the main text is based on an extant manuscript (uncredited) from the Rudolf Steiner House library in London. It was edited by Eileen Lloyd, with further checks against the German made by Paul Breslaw, Paul V. O'Leary and others, to whom we are grateful. Any remaining errors or omissions are the responsibility of the publishers. Special thanks go to Johanna Collis for her excellent translation of the additional material by Andreas Bracher.

S.E.G., September 2014

---

[*] Preface to *Hitler's Table Talk*, New York 2000.

Preface

Since the end of the 1960s there has been a huge growth in literature about Hitler. The reasons for this are many. With the increasing distance in time, sources have become more accessible and there remains a need to work through this phase of German history. Furthermore, the theme proved to be popular and lucrative for publishers. Other things are more difficult to weigh up but must be added, in particular an obscurely felt summons to come to grips with the forces of destruction that broke out during the era of National Socialism — in order to unravel the tasks for the future.

Professional historians as well as outsiders to the profession have researched and interpreted the phenomenon of National Socialism. Karl-Dietrich Bracher, Emil Nolte and Hans-Adolf Jacobsen have submitted their extensive analyses. Journalists of note, like Konrad Heiden and Hermann Rauschning, published their astonishing reports during Hitler's lifetime and have been quoted again and again. American and British historians and émigré German scholars have grappled with the task of studying the twelve years of dictatorship in a scientific manner. Then Werner Maser came up with the claim that he was able to describe Hitler's life 'without gaps', thanks to new sources of material. Joachim Fest's biography was recognized by professional historians as exhaustive commentary on Hitler's background and modus operandi. Of course, no one raised the question as to whether one should talk about a 'biography' in the first place, since this would presuppose the working of spirituality in the realm of the true ego. Those familiar with Hitler experienced the intangible, spectral nature of his being in daily intercourse with him. Memoirs from some of those involved at that time establish this fact, most notably Albert Speer, for whom Hitler became, in retrospect, an 'historical abstraction'. In his attempt to analyse Hitler, Carl Friedrich von Weizsäcker notes that Hitler 'never was a *real* person'.

With all this in mind, it becomes clear that research has circled back to the starting point, to what had already been achieved by Heiden and Rauschning. Compendia of sources are put together, the beginnings of Hitlerism are illuminated, contemporary entanglements are sorted out, detailed information is piled up, and brilliant interpretations are formulated regarding the world-political and social dynamics which destroyed Europe's historical order and brought about such moral tragedy. But, in its basic outlines, the overall picture has hardly been altered. One almost has the feeling that the overabundance of material hinders one's understanding instead of helping it. Anyone who lived through the years 1933–1945 with a keen sense for historical realities starts to wonder about the historical comprehension of many of the authors. Clearly, they fail to perceive the fact that, in the twentieth century, modern consciousness stepped over a threshold in the history of consciousness. If reality in its totality, meaning also the dimension of spiritual forces, is to come into the field of vision, this threshold must be crossed. Thus, the critical examination of reality requires a complementary method that allows one to discern the intervention of the motivating forces of history.

As with human actions, historical developments have a symbolic character and communicate themselves in the form of 'speechless speech'. Their meaning becomes clear when the historical process is perceived as the physiognomic expression of spiritual forces, just as a human biography must be understood as the unfolding and display of the essence of the individual ego. Historical events must be seen as symptoms and ordered accordingly.

Rudolf Steiner's anthroposophical spiritual science has developed a method which opens the door to a sphere of objective spiritual reality. For the person who follows its indications, a sense of reality becomes instilled which leads to a perception of the whole *gestalt*. Facts become transparent through the formative forces at work, the spiritual background comes to the fore, and the occult aspect reveals itself.

Rudolf Steiner noted very early on the forces of destruction which announced themselves in the Hitler-movement. The focus of the essay which follows is on these forces, at whose disposal the well-known functionaries placed themselves while the bedazzled masses lay low. We will ask at which point in history the adversaries erupted, what their methods were, and the meaning and nature of their substance. In the course of our investigation it became clear that we now need to see through the twelve-year tyranny if we intend to bring about a free ordering of society corresponding to the present level of human evolution. Certainly, this is also the implication of C.F. von Weizsäcker's assumption that a connection exists between this most important unresolved problem in our past and the unsolved future problems of the world. Insight into the past can lead to social relationships which will hinder future attacks by the enemies of freedom and — using the criteria of humanity derived from anthroposophy — will guarantee the free space necessary for the development of individuality.

These accounts appear in the form in which they were presented on St John's Day, 1966, to members of the Anthroposophical Society. Since then they have been distributed in manuscript form. Stylistic revisions were made for printing the German edition, and a Preface has been added to establish the connection with the current state of research.

1. The Third Reich

The attempt to ask a few questions about the occult aspects of National Socialism needs some preparation. In view of the difficulties of the subject it will be necessary to develop hypotheses to a certain extent before provisional conclusions can be reached. No more can be expected from this than a shop-floor inventory, so as to permeate the materials put at our disposal by contemporary historical research with the ideas of anthroposophical spiritual science. The phenomenon we are investigating — National Socialism — resembles an iceberg. Only part of the real contour is visible; the major part remains under water. Our task also consists in taking into account those parts which, in a manner of speaking, are under water, i.e. to complete the observation so as to include its hidden aspects.

The following delineations are intended as the beginning of an education in cognition. It is a matter of the conscious ego taking hold of the historical reality which clusters around the year 1933, in order to master the future and to make it possible to see through the enemy — no matter what mask he may be wearing. St John's Day can encourage us in this. For, as Rudolf Steiner put it in the well-known Saint John's imagination, there appears at this time of year, 'as in the warning appearance of Uriel ... historical conscience which is particularly ill-developed in the present time'. At this time of St John we can feel the urge to widen and deepen historical conscience, the urge to create a sweeping, far-reaching historical consciousness out of a body of opinions which often neglects historical realities.

This call gets steadily louder and more distinct. Many will remember an example from political theatre, Peter Weiss's play *The Investigation*, which depicts the Auschwitz trials.[*] The effect

---

[*] The trials took place in Frankfurt between 1963 and 1965. The play premiered in October 1965.

on the public (young people for the most part) was unusual. A deep bewilderment and mute meditation spread through the audience. Many symptoms present themselves to the observer and indicate unmistakeably that a 'deadline' is near. In 1966 it has been 33 years since that other world erupted in Germany. Thirty-three years amounts to one generation.

At Christmas 1917 Steiner presented for the first time the results of his spiritual-scientific research on the meaning of the 33-year rhythm in the life of Jesus. A rhythm, or cycle, was found there, a connection was established between two events which lie 33 years apart. In the starting year (the 'Christmas year'), of the cycle a seed is planted which resurrects in the final year of this historical rhythm – the Easter year. This works for good as well as for evil. (This rhythm is not found in the events of personal life, where the laws of karma govern.) As Steiner said in his lecture of 23 December 1917 (CW 180),[*] 'Et Incarnatus est', 'All things in historical developments rise from the grave in transfigured form'. If we apply this to our problem, we find the effects of the events of 1933 rising up in 1966. In the spirit of this 33-year cyclical evolution of historical events, and looking forward to the turn of the century, it is now up to us to make our impact by undertaking the task of understanding the real causes and motives which caused the German people (the 'Ego-folk' of Central Europe) to be the first to plunge into the abyss of evil, and then to act in accordance with this knowledge.

This exercise in cognition can only be performed in the manner of the twentieth century, in so far as we attempt to show the interaction of supersensible forces with physical events. Humanity has begun developments for which it still lacks the necessary concepts. If we are to decipher the scripture of the events, concepts must be forged which take into account the supersensible dimension. Historical science as it is practised today has been left behind at the cognitive level of the nineteenth century, for it cannot yet recognize the impact of concrete spiritual forces upon historical developments.

---

[*] CW = Collected Works (*Gesamtausgabe* or 'GA' in German) of Rudolf Steiner.

Anyone familiar with the present and with the demands of the future in the twentieth century will have noticed the various forms assumed by *concrete* evil. Rudolf Steiner has shed light on the riddle of evil, its supersensible power, and has described its dual nature. Only if we distinguish evil in the moral realm from evil in the practical realm, the luciferic from the ahrimanic, can we gain access to the problems of the present. Historical investigations can take their orientation from spiritual-scientific perception.

We are grateful to our colleagues in the field of history, whose example has been an inspiration: to Walter Johannes Stein, the first history teacher at the Stuttgart Waldorf School in 1919, and to Emil Bock, whose historical presentation encouraged our own venture. The unrivalled model remains the *The Karma of Untruthfulness* Vols. I & II (CW 173 & 174) which Steiner presented at Dornach at the turn of the year 1916/17. These meditations prepared his own intervention in the political developments of the epochal year 1917, in so far as he sketched there for the first time the concept of the 'threefold social order',[*] a new social order corresponding to the level of evolution of contemporary humanity, whose dynamic centre is the free spiritual life, the cultural realm freed from governmental control.

One remark about sources. This presentation is based upon the author's own experience of the historical reality between 1933 and 1945. It takes into account the collected surveys by American, English and German authors and uses, as far as possible, the results of Steiner's spiritual-scientific research. Finally, the author wishes to acknowledge with thanks the exchanges with experts and friends, Friedrich Häusler and Günter Schubert.

We will now try to move the phenomenon of National Socialism into the field of vision and grasp it in a spirit of contemplative discernment, where thinking turns into seeing. I will draw upon an article by Emil Bock[1] and quote from it at length.

---

[*]This refers to Rudolf Steiner's ideas regarding the social ordering of society. See further in Rudolf Steiner, *Towards Social Renewal*, London 1999.

Four weeks before the Nazi seizure of power, on the night of 27 February 1933, the destruction of the Berlin Reichstag took place. The Session Chamber went up in flames. The gigantic cupola acted like a chimney. Witnesses testified that the whole hall went up in flames all at once. This took place a few days before the decisive elections of March 1933, during a situation of great political tension and general nervousness. At the time, a rumour was circulating, noted by Count Kessler in his journal, that a fake murder attempt was being planned against the head of the National Socialist Party, in order to create a pretext to launch an attack against the Communist Party. It will be necessary at this point to bring clearly to mind the image of night fire, the visual and acoustic experience of the flaring, crackling blaze, in order to measure what took place in the souls of the spectators. Anybody who has had occasion to see entire streets burn down when cities were bombed, as we did during World War II, will know the fascination of unfettered, elemental storms of destruction.

It doesn't add much to raise the question of responsibility. While the well-known series of articles in *Der Spiegel* made for animated scholarly discussions about the Reichstag fire, they didn't solve the problem. The investigation succeeded no further than describing the full use of fire expertise, criminological and pyrotechnical analyses and the construction of various theories about the author of the crime.

Let us stick to overt facts. At 11.30 p.m., the Session Chamber bursts into flames. The main characters of the drama meet at the site of the fire. We are told about choleric outbursts by the 'Leader' (who is really the 'Led'), his raging about Communist 'subhumans', and his stated intention to hang all Communist deputies in the Reichstag.

The Reichstag fire provides the overture to the twelve years of Nazi rule. It contains in one single symbolic appearance the motif of conflagration which will dominate the whole horizon in the last act of the drama. Whoever analyses the process encounters a disparity between the intentions of those pulling the strings and the avalanche-like consequences of their actions. A vent is pulled open and a whole world of lurking spirits of destruction breaks in, takes hold of peoples' darkened consciousness and does its annihilating work in uncontrolled, instinctual actions and semi-schizophrenic compulsiveness.

There is an interesting description of this process in a scholarly history. I quote here from Hans Mommsen's book on the Reichstag fire and its consequences:[2]

> The night of the fire, Hitler passed abruptly into a phase of totalitarian experiments, whereas until then he had steered a moderate, pseudo-legal course, although terrorist activity by the SS and the SA was, of course, growing. The next day's emergency decree anticipated in the form of a coup the seizure of all parliamentary powers. The decree had not been planned, but was made possible by the nervous impatience with which the political leadership reacted to the imagined Communist counter-coup. Obviously, a moderate Chancellor of the Reich did not turn overnight into a power-drunk dictator, but the hysterical exaggeration which led to the fire of 27 February helped to do away with his last inhibitions and delivered him altogether to the dynamics of dictatorship.

The emergency decree makes clear what had been meant. Basic rights which had been guaranteed by the Weimar Constitution were suspended. Arbitrary searches of apartments, arbitrary imprisonment of 'troublemakers', the dissolution of political parties, associations and meetings, the confiscation of property — all these became possible.

There was no legal protection against such abuses. Through this decree a development ended that had started in 1215 during the Crusades with the great foundation of freedom — the Magna Carta. Now the great charter of un-freedom is prepared, and illegality begins to prevail in Germany.

'With the opening of this underground vent, a whole flood of deception and mischief pours out on to the stage of events.' Thus does Emil Bock characterize the development. The world of bourgeois order is finished; the breakdown of central-European humanity begins. The paralysis of consciousness and the default of consciousness starts here. At this point, this other world closes in on Germany, to reign there for twelve years. It was beaten . . . but never overcome.

The bloodbath of 20 June 1934 is an important step in the process which started in 1933, namely the disempowerment of the SA and the stepping forward of the SS—symbolically represented as the victory of the black colour of the SS over the brown of the SA. The chief of staff of the SA, a mercenary at heart, represents de-civilization of the first degree, which manifests as the unleashing of forces arising from instincts and passions, as moral corruption. Here we observe evil in the realm of morality. With the SS chief, whose mask-like opacity also covers up his individual insignificance, we have the appearance on stage of anonymity personified. De-civilization of the second degree begins, and can be equated with a radical increase of dehumanization and 'de-souling' (soul-lessness)— the eradication of heart forces. With the help of the Gestapo and its apparatus, the SS will lead the satanic-ahrimanic machinery of death and destruction to a triumph of annihilation. Thus, the domination of the soulless spirit (working spiritually through the denial of spiritual reality) was able to be established, having been freed from all moral inhibitions and humane considerations. And this spirit proceeds like a gigantic spider who wraps its web around its victims and paralyses them, so that they let themselves be overpowered and make no resistance. An analysis of the events of 1934 shows the same thing that occurred at the time of the Reichstag fire. There are no conscious plans; the men at the forefront of events have no thoughts or, at best, quite muddled ones. The eyewitness Gisevius, a member of the resistance movement, speaks of a 'kaleidoscope of inadequacies'.

Once again we see taking place what Rudolf Steiner observed at the outbreak of war in 1914: through a darkened, clouded human consciousness, non-human beings work their way into history. Human weaknesses serve as the gate through which they sally forth. Covered by the stage-setting of outer events, a monstrous consciousness-vacuum exerts its hellish suctional power. The idling motion of a whole epoch leads to the point

where the ground opens up and an anonymous will of unfore-
seeable proportions arises.

Let us take a glance to the end. This so-called Third Reich
lasted twelve years and three months—five years and eight
months of war, and six years and seven months of so-called
peace. The conflagration which started on 27 February 1933 now
fills the whole stage. Something ghostly covers the whole scene
in March 1945. The Russians have penetrated into a bombed-out
Berlin. The 'Led' has taken refuge in the underground command
centre—the Bunker—in the garden of the ruined Reich Chan-
cellery. Visitors describe the breakdown of his forces, which can
only be kept up through drugs and his doctors' injections. The
English historian Alan Bullock characterizes this final stage in
the following words: 'His deeper being, the brutal hatred, the
arrogance, the vengefulness came to the fore without disguise.'
For him, the ending of his own life was the end of all things. Now
Death reigns. He gives orders to complete the destruction, con-
demns his earlier trusted doctor, has prisoners executed, has his
own brother-in-law killed, demands the death of his besieged
soldiers and finally destroys himself.

The decree of 19 March 1945, later called the Nero Decree, is
witness to this will to destroy. To quote: 'All military transporta-
tion, news, industry and medical installation, as well as all real
assets on Reich territory that the enemy could use in any way to
pursue the fight, either immediately or in the foreseeable future,
must be destroyed.' This meant the annihilation of all industrial
installations, all important electric, water and gas works, postal
and radio installations, and the creation of a complete transpor-
tation desert. The population was to be forcibly evacuated on foot
to central Germany. It is hard to imagine the catastrophe that
would have resulted. In the case of Stuttgart, all industry was to be
destroyed, all tramways, the whole fleet of vehicles, all news
installations, all bakeries, all slaughterhouses, etc. That it didn't
happen is due to the resistance of the then mayor of the city and the
initiative of a few individuals. While they couldn't stop the
destruction of the bridge over the Neckar, they were able to save
the Berger Steg bridge, which guaranteed the town's water supply.

This 'Nero Decree' was designed to bring about the total annihilation of the Germans by their own head of state. Such ideas of destruction had surfaced quite early. Conversations with Hermann Rauschning in 1932,[3] then president of the Danzig senate, elicited the following: 'We will never capitulate. We may be destroyed, but we will take with us the whole world: Muspilli, the burning of the world.' The word originated in Germanic heritage: Muspilli ... world destruction in blood and fire.

A few additional remarks about the walk-on cast. It should not be seen as a whim that no specific names are mentioned here. We will speak about the 'Leader' as 'the Led', and call him 'the Medium' (the comparison will be clarified in the last chapter). Actually, his birthplace (Braunau) was considered a centre for mediums. Impartial observers have noticed the 'medium' element there.

Rauschning describes the 'Led' in the following words: 'One is forced to think of mediums. Most of the time they are perfectly ordinary, insignificant people. Suddenly, forces fall upon them as if from the skies, which elevate them far above the ordinary measure. These forces have no relation to their ordinary personalities. They are like visitors from another planet. The medium is possessed. When the spell breaks, he reverts to his ordinariness.' Otto Strasser, one of the earliest National Socialists to oppose Hitler, explains: 'a sleepwalker — truly a medium, as the most chaotic epochs of human history bring them to the fore. He emerges from the penumbra, between night and day ... The medium sinks into a trance when he meets the public.' To quote François-Poncet,[4] the French ambassador to Berlin: 'He fell into a kind of trance. His facial expression was one of ecstatic rapture.'

To complete his own nothingness, the Medium surrounds himself — I follow here Folkert Wilken's conclusions — with three figures, which stand like mirror images: a Minister of Propaganda and Popular Enlightenment, enhancing the 'head-man'[*] in

---

[*] These terms refer to Rudolf Steiner's threefold picture of the nature of the human being, comprising functions of thinking (head), feeling (heart) and will (metabolism). See further in *The Study of Man*, Sussex 2004.

the Medium; a Marshall of the Empire, a caricature of the 'chest-man'; the SS Chief and the Head of the Police, enhancing jointly the chaotic 'limb-man'.[5] The Minister of Propaganda, minted from a Mephistophelian mould down to his physical appearance, is the representative of the intellectual citizen type. He takes care of corrupting the thinking of the masses through his weekly paper *Das Reich*, where he regularly writes the editorial. The Marshall stands at the top of the military apparatus. His urge to show off and his infantilism were as well-known as his artistic thefts and his amorality. He described himself as the last Renaissance man of the twentieth century. The SS Chief appears as the fossilised representative of the party's will, a cold fanatic of destruction. He is responsible for the construction of the SS State, which was to be directed by the Black Order — the Order of Pure Blood, the biological elite. The goal of this SS State was the 'new breeding of the German master-race in the great German *Lebensraum*'. Three institutions were built according to this plan: the military institution, in the Waffen-SS; the institution for murder, in the Central Office for the Security of the Reich, which gained the responsibility for the annihilation of European Jewry, the 'final solution'; and, the Institute of Breeding in *Lebensborn* (this organization was to take care of the Aryanizing of the German people, through 'helpers of procreation' and 'marriages of popular interest'). In this state, political rule was shored up by the 'three sinister companions, Force, Fear and Passion'.

How does historical science interpret the phenomenon of National Socialism today?[6] What answer does it give to the question of its historical roots? There are two opposing views, which go more or less as follows. National Socialism supposedly descended upon the Germans like a sudden natural catastrophe, an event that could not have been averted and which lacked any foundation or preparation in the German past. This reading leads to an overvaluation of the Medium, a gigantic overestimate of his historical responsibility and guilt, and ends with a psychological scrutiny of his troubled youth and his abnormal character traits. Thus, for instance, the historian Herzfeld describes National Socialism as a 'revolutionary culmination of the exception'. Over against this ahistorical image of the demon, who destroys a world which was connected with him by nothing more than coincidence, there stands another interpretation. National Socialism, when seen as the almost logical outcome of German heritage, would seem to be a negative version of the completion of the nation's history. By way of proof, historical lines of development are traced as follows: a power-political one from Frederick the Great through Bismarck to the Led; a spiritual-historical one from Luther's *Obrigkeitsfrommheit*[7] through Hegel's divinization of the State, to Rosenberg's 'myth'.[8] The most effective representation of this point of view is offered by the American publicist William L. Shirer, whose two-volume book *The Rise and Fall of the Third Reich* has become a bestseller.

These explanations have been attacked. It has been pointed out with good reason that history is neither an uninterrupted stream nor a succession of unrelated volcanic eruptions. The notion of a continuum does not make it possible to understand a phenomenon like the National Socialist dynamic in its historical meaning, which breaks the continuity. The phenomenon of National Socialism can only be understood as an occurrence with universal historical value. Ever since 1917, the year of the Bolshevik Revolution, there has been a visible crisis of liberal democratic states. Developments took place that can no longer be mastered with blueprints from the old, conservative style. The landslide began then, in 1917. In many places in Europe, Fascist dictatorial tendencies became active—in Italy, in Eastern Europe, in the Iberian peninsula.

One might also think of the erosion of the Weimar Republic, or even of later developments in the Federal Republic of Germany, in the light of Karl Jaspers' book *Wohin treibt die Bundesrepublik?*, ('Whither the Federal Republic?')[9] where he pointed out that West Germany could slide into cold dictatorship on its way to a party oligarchy.

But it is not enough simply to lay bare the individual root fibres of National Socialism. One must understand the whole rootstock out of which this historical reality grew up. It goes back to the materialistic worldview or—to refine the idea further—to the biological-naturalistic thinking which culminated in Darwinism in the nineteenth century. Darwin's theory of evolution dominated the cognitive life of the last century. This scientific conception of the human being did not lead *out* through the animal kingdom but only understood man in so far as he was animal in nature. One example can be found in the sense theory, the doctrine about human senses, where the higher senses — the sense of language, the sense of thinking, the ego-sense — were not taken into consideration. It was left to Rudolf Steiner to discover the higher senses, where humanness is grounded. There was no adequate science of man. The consequence of a theory which classifies the human being scientifically within the animal order is obvious. As Emil Bock put it: the animal theory became demon theory.[10] The theory became praxis. Through man the animal revealed itself. The demonic elements of animal-like sentiments came to the foreground. Those who still had a hold of religious tradition, like Rauschning, said: it is the eruption of the Beast.

The author of the Apocalypse, standing at the edge of land and sea, the border of two worlds, describes the rising of the Adversary in two forms. He watches a monster rise out of the waters of the sea, a beast with seven heads and ten horns. From the hard, solid land he sees another beast rise up. It is inconspicuous and could easily be confused with a lamb. It is the two-horned beast, hard as steel — cold power.

Were one to ask for the most ominous visible expression of National Socialist rule, one could point to the monstrous blood offering, rising to the millions. The representatives of this rule wanted to change life. They served gods to whom they offered the youth of their own land, to whom they wanted to offer a whole group of mankind, European Jewry. Historical examination must look at the terror and its escalation — the intimidation, the moral subjugation, the physical destruction. Terrorism and revolution have always come together. Let us but remember the terror of the French Revolution, whose best known representative was Robespierre. In Germany, political terror had never or barely taken place before the Great War. Political terror on the street, in organizations like the Feme and similar ones, started after the First World War. Their model may have been provided by anarchist examples. Erzberger and Rathenau were assassinated, and in May 1922 an attempt was made against Rudolf Steiner's life in Munich. Open terror reigned until 9 November 1938, the infamous *Kristallnacht* ('Night of Broken Glass'), when Jewish property was destroyed and citizens were brutalized. Secret terror raged in concentration camps and extermination camps. Here a system was formed that was frightening in its efficiency and perfection. In this case, historical roots might be found in Philip the Fair's trial of the Knights Templar.

Research has shown that, as a rule, the perpetrators of this terror were neither criminals nor fanatics. When in the course of the famous Nuremberg trials they stood in front of their judges, they described themselves as 'small guys' in a gigantic system of destruction. What is the characteristic of these actors? The loss of a personal 'centre', the loss of an ego. They are hollowed men, instruments of radical evil, products of a system of technical and bureaucratic functioning that aims at the eradication of the ego, an institution that is full of ahrimanic spirit. In such an institution the individual no longer has any responsibility; he simply executes the purpose of the assigned task without asking any questions. This ego-less man is the raw material out of which the handymen and henchmen of terror are formed. Reduced to being mere parts of the techno-rational apparatus, such people have become indoctrinated robots, to use an expression from scholarly literature.

What about the self-image and contemporary interpretation of the dictatorship which began in 1933? The concept 'Third Reich' (Third Empire) was applied to it. Its popular construction went as follows. After the First Reich (the Holy Roman Empire of the German Nation), which lasted from 962 to 1806 – almost a thousand years – there followed a short-lived Empire of Bismarck, founded in 1871 and lasting till 1918. After the interlude of the Weimar Republic, the Third Empire – the time of the 'system' as the Brown despots called it – started in 1933 and, according to its founder, it would last a thousand years. It turned into a twelve-year hellish spectre instead.

Many contemporaries felt that after the first third of the twentieth century a new historical epoch was being proclaimed. In his conversations with Rauschning, the Medium declared that the Age of Reason—a dead end of the spirit—had ended. With his movement, presumably, the Middle Ages were coming to an end. From now on it would be essential to have magical vision. The assumption was that this would be the direction of human development. A colossal transformation of human nature was in progress, the new man was living among us, fearless and fierce. There is no point in interpreting these statements, which appear as terrible distortions of reality.

These notions had been met half-way by the conservative Moeller van den Bruck's book *The Third Reich*, which appeared after the First World War and popularized the concept. Books on historical developments since 1933 have claimed that the concept originated in an ancient mystical realm. The chief witness to this mystical tradition is Joachim of Fiore, an abbot from Calabria in southern Italy at the time of the Hohenstaufen.[*] Lessing refers to the Calabrese monk without naming him in his *Education of the Human Race*, in the closing examination of the third step of spiritual development, the age of the Holy Spirit. And Schelling introduces him in his *Philosophy of Revelation*, which culminates in his description of three epochs of Christianity: the Petrine epoch, the Pauline epoch and a Johannine epoch, which is the crowning glory of history.

Little is known about the life of the southern Italian Joachim, who is still venerated today as a great prophet in the little town of San Giovanni in Fiore, where he is buried. But the principal motifs of his biography are easily identifiable. Born in 1145, Joachim was forty years younger than St Francis of Assisi. He was well educated in the Norman kingdom of Sicily, and was brought to the court of King Roger at Palermo, at that time a nodal point of all cultural streams. As the heir of the Vikings, Roger reigned over his Normans, over the conquered Muslim

---

[*] House of Hohenstaufen was a dynasty of German monarchs reigning from 1138 to 1254.

Saracens, over many Greeks and Jews in the islands to the East, and over the Lombards who had emigrated from Italy. No religious propaganda was allowed in his kingdom. Arabic learning and art were shining here. The most famous medical school of the times was located in Salerno. Here, according to Hartmann's 'Legend',[*] Knight Henry sought a cure for leprosy from an Arabic authority. A giant silver map of the then-known world was made in Roger's kingdom. He commissioned the Arabic scholar Edrisi to write a cosmography. Joachim spent his youth in this land, where East and West meet, on Greek soil occupied by the Arabic spirit and ruled by the Norman nobility.

There then followed a pilgrimage to the Holy Land. There is talk of a mystical experience on Mount Carmel, the important site in the life of the prophet Elijah. But the figure of Joachim still remains unclear. It was only after his return to his homeland that the contours become clearer. He spent three days and three nights fasting and praying in a cave near a Greek monastery at Mount Etna. At that point he heard an inner voice that pointed him to Calabria. Then came the resolve: I will only serve the King of Kings. He started to preach out of the fullness of his inner soul, was induced to join the Cistercian order and soon after was elected Abbot. He then built his own hermitage and founded the Order of San Giovanni of Fiore, which lasted 150 years and then merged into the Cistercian order.

His decisive inner experience occurred around the year 1190. The breakthrough took place in the early hours of the night before Pentecost. Joachim describes it as follows: 'As I awoke from my sleep around morning prayer [the nightly vigil from midnight to 3 o'clock], I took this book [i.e. St John's Apocalypse] for my meditation. Then suddenly, at the hour when our lion resurrected from the tribe of Judah, the light of knowledge drove through my spiritual eyes, and the fullness of this book was revealed to me.' The illumination of this instant brought Joachim to the end of many years' wrestling with the

---

[*] *Der arme Heinrich* ('Poor Heinrich') by Hartmann von Aue, a Middle High German narrative poem, probably written in the 1190s.

meaning of Holy Scripture and of the course of history as described here.

Out of the many studies about Joachim, I would like to select *Ewiges Evangelium* by Wolfgang Schickler, which was published in 1937 and contains important information. In his philosophical publication *Weltgeschichte und Heilgeschehen* ('World History and Healing Events'), published in 1953, Karl Löwith[11] places Joachim among those connected with great ideas. But the decisive understanding of Joachim was brought by Rudolf Steiner in his cycle of lectures on *The Apocalypse of St John* (CW 104) and his farewell lecture cycle in England, *True And False Paths In Spiritual Investigation* (CW 243).[12] The most intimate indications are given in the descriptions in the English cycle. There we see Joachim before us as a great initiate in the sense of the Middle Ages, named in connection with the teachers of Chartres and with Brunetto Latini, Dante's teacher. His countenance is drawn in a tragic vein, which talks about the loss of the old mysteries. But the finely veined, sinewy hands are testimony that the abbot is ready to dig for the secrets which have fallen away from his cognition.

Joachim developed the results of his meditative research in three main works. Let us mention here the key themes: the teaching about three epochs, according to which history fulfils itself in a three-step evolution: the message of the Eternal Gospel, which is read in the spirit before it is spelled out; the hope that cognition will progress to what he calls *intellectus spiritualis*, a spiritualized thinking that becomes seeing; and the proclamation of the *Novus Dux*, the messianic Leader who will accomplish spiritual renewal (Löwith takes for granted that the spiritual title 'Dux' was later transferred to Italy to the political leader, Il Duce of Fascism).

Joachim's teaching of the three epochs became the most significant; it refers to the gradual unfolding of the human being in the course of historical development. For Joachim, history became a pilgrimage of human *becoming*, in theological terms a self-realization, unfolding and representation of the trinity of the Godhead. This marks the beginning of true historical examination. Joachim distinguishes three epochs: the world-epoch of the Father, lasting from the beginning of the world to the incarnation of the Saviour; the world-epoch of the Son, lasting until the year 1260 and comprising 42 generations; and the world-epoch of the Holy Spirit, which will last until the end of the world.

One can illustrate the tripartite description of historical epochs by looking at the stages of human biography. The first third of life is when a person learns his karmic preconditions and inheritance—through his time and place, his birth, his physical constitution, his soul disposition and his spiritual orientation. This stands, as it were, under the sign of the Father. The second third of life leads to a transformation of the soul and to the formation of the parts of the soul. Friendship and love, work and profession are found during this time, when the work of the Son will unfold. The last third of life can become the epoch of spiritual completion, when one may succeed in realizing the meaning of his incarnation, and give form to his archetypal themes—as Mörike[13] puts it, 'by breaking the seal of the Gospel of his destiny'.

Joachim speaks about the three stages of development in an imaginative style, which is full of picturesque expressions. The secrets of Holy Scripture point us to three worldly conditions. In the first phase we stand under the Law; in the second stage we live under Grace; in the third stage, which we expect in the near future, even richer Grace will be offered. The first condition is related to the Father; the second to the Son; the third to the Holy Spirit. The first condition is the servitude of slaves; the second is the service of sons; the third is that of love. The first is the status of servants; the second that of free men; the third that of friends. The first brings grass; the second shows standing blades; the third provides wheat. The ascent of the three ages corresponds to a growing independence of the human being. The most significant conquest of the third age will be the *intellectus spiritualis*—thinking turned into the eye of the spirit.

The third kingdom appears as the kingdom of the manifestation of the Coming—more precisely, the Coming One. The third kingdom should be the time of rebirth in the spirit—the epoch referred to in Scripture as the Parousia, the return of Christ in the clouds. In that epoch, the Gospel will become unmediated learning. What is written in the Scriptures will become living reality. Then the time of deciphering Scripture, letter by letter, will be over. The Eternal Gospel will come to human souls as historical reality.

Rudolf Steiner became the herald of this teaching of the three epochs when, over Christmas 1923, he gave a grand interpretation of history in his cycle of lectures *World History in the Light of Anthroposophy* (CW 233). There he shows that the usual division between Antiquity, the Middle Ages and the Modern Age calls forth false representations. Instead we must distinguish the truly ancient segment of history, which can only be grasped imaginatively — the old temple culture of Asia and Egypt, the epoch of magical spirituality where man was still equipped with godly attributes. This segment lasts until the burning of the temple at Ephesus, that is, until the birth of Alexander the Great in 356 BC. Then comes the second epoch which embraces Rome, the Middle Ages and extends up to the immediate present. This epoch covers the two millennia after Christ, a time of disinheritance and wandering through the wilderness, but also the time of forming the ego and freedom. Then the third world, the third epoch, will start.[14]

We understand this third epoch as the epoch of the renewal of the mysteries, when spirituality will be recreated after the necessary loss of the old godly forces. This world-age was brought about by modern spiritual science, whose students we can become. On the threshold of this third age stands the Novus Dux, the New Leader, with his message: the third world has begun, the time of revelation for the Coming One, the resurrection in the spirit.

On the last day of the Christmas Conference, on 1 January 1924, Rudolf Steiner said: 'This Christmas Conference must be a night of vigil, a feast of worldwide epochal change which we must dedicate and devote ourselves to in the cultivation of spiritual life.' This worldwide, epochal change, which Rudolf Steiner spoke about after the dedication of the new Society grounded in the spirit is, in Joachim's words, the 'third kingdom', the kingdom of the redeeming and healing spirit. The frightening shadows, the counter-image of the light-filled new beginning, are also appearing on the stage of history.

We can now understand the phrase noted by the historian Karl Heyer in an autobiographical sketch written shortly before his death in 1964, that National Socialism is nothing other than the 'anti-anthroposophical movement'.

2. The Sign

The conclusion one has to draw is that the political reality of those twelve years must be seen as the counter-image (anti-type) of what spiritual history calls the 'third kingdom'. The third kingdom is a concept from the history of the mysteries. History becomes mystery-history when the spiritual guidance of humanity is recognized, when the intervention of cosmic powers is revealed, when a person views himself as part of a divine evolution. Whoever speaks of the third kingdom speaks of history in a trinitarian way. We owe this to the great Joachim of Fiore. St Paul can be counted as his predecessor, when he distinguished an age of natural law, an age of the written Jewish law and an age of the evangelical law which is disclosed through the world's Saviour.

A famous saying is attributed to the abbot Joachim: 'Whoever learns to pray can become a priest or even a bishop. Whoever studies the law can become a cardinal or even aspire to the papacy. Whoever studies the Bible can become a heretic.' Joachim's life was spent in prayer and in studying the Bible. Therefore, it is not surprising that he ended up among the ranks of the great heretics, as his teachings were misunderstood by some of his followers. Thus, in the fourteenth century the Roman popular tribune Cola di Rienzi (the hero of Wagner's first great opera) played the role of Novus Dux. (In his youth the Medium, i.e. Hitler, identified with this figure.) Others, like Francis of Assisi, were also designated as such.

Six hundred years later, the philosophers of German Idealism picked up Joachim's ideas. A break with tradition then followed in the nineteenth century when the idea of the 'third kingdom' was secularized and brought on to the political stage. There it was taken up by the journalist Moeller van den Bruck, who made it possible for the rulers of 1933 to see themselves as representatives of a 'third kingdom'. Van den Bruck himself has been shown to have been influenced by the Russian Konstantin Merezhkovsky, who stands in the direct line of succession from the German Idealists. Thus, the spiritual lines of descent are interwoven.

What happened on the political scene between 1933 and 1945 was an atavistic backsliding into the condition of the 'first age' as Joachim had characterized it. Human beings submitted themselves to the Law. They were reduced to servitude and were disciplined by the whip, became childishly immature and lived in the soul disposition of fear. The powers of dark, brutish regression appear in the mask and form of National Socialism. These are the counter-images mentioned by Rudolf Steiner in his lecture of 9 October 1918, *The Work of the Angels in Man's Astral Body* (CW 182). Because a deadline was missed, new spiritual possibilities were left untouched, and evil (non-spirit, anti-spirit) was able to break in. The whole movement which resurfaced in 1933 must be understood as a problem of 'vacuum' — it was sucked in by a space void of ideas. It is not accurately understood as a 'pressure-problem', as is usually the case, caused by economic pressures, political decline, and the cultural decadence after the First World War. Karl Heyer already expressed this fact in the title of his notable book on National Socialism, *Wenn die Götter den Tempel verlassen* ('When the Gods Abandon the Temple') (1947), which could conclude with the words — 'then the demons move in'.

The third world-age is the time of the revelation of the Coming, whose return Rudolf Steiner first announced in 1910. In his lectures on the appearance of Christ in the etheric world, he points precisely to the year 1933. Ever since then, the first sign of a new capacity, the etheric event, 'the most important development in the world', has been visible. But at the same time, the huge diversionary manoeuvres of the adversary appear on stage. Instead of an illumination of consciousness, a darkening of consciousness took place. Instead of a fulfilment of the spirit, there was an evacuation of the spirit, a void of spirit.

We will assign three code names on history's chapter for 1933: 'The Third Reich', the Sign and Klingsor. The name Klingsor points to the spiritual battlefield which will be described at the end of this presentation. First we must speak about the Sign, the emblem of National Socialism.

We start with a thought developed by Rudolf Steiner on 4 June 1924 when speaking to workmen at the Goetheanum,[1] prior to his departure to teach the 'Agriculture Course' at Koberwitz. These lectures for the workers of the Goetheanum, from which members of the Anthroposophical Society were excluded, stand out by the courage of their words and the concreteness of their pronouncements. They are addressed to listeners who have not been spoiled by intellectualism and who address their questions directly. When a question was asked about Freemasonry and its purpose, Rudolf Steiner answered as follows. Today's Free-masonry is but a shadow of what it once was. But it is still possible to see in the outer forms of Masonry its mystery background, the last traces of a tradition leading back far into the past. In olden days, mystery students had to travel long distances to visit the mystery sites. It took them a shorter time than it would take for people today, for they had more stamina and tired less easily. First of all their development consisted in an education of their sensations, a refining and cultivation of their feelings. As a result, men of a similar rank recognized each other upon first meeting through their handshake. This grasp showed that the other person had finer sensations. The second means of recognition was the Sign. Rudolf Steiner explained how such signs arose out of the further development of bodily gestures related to sensations, for instance the gestures that mean 'I understand' or 'this does not concern me', or 'we understand each other well'. A complete sign language was thus developed as a natural language accessible to the mystery initiate, a making-visible of the inner man, the rune-like expression of soul forces and movements. Language became the third sign of recognition. One must remember here that in earlier times language was not just common chit-chat, but rather a religious act. World-speech had not fallen as deep as it has now, when languages have turned almost exclusively into the means of transmitting external information and banal understandings. The different qualities of the vowels, which mirror our feeling and will, and of the consonants, which describe the external world, were still perceived. Every mystery student, no matter what his origin, perceived the reality that is pictured in the sounds EL. E: I feel a tremor of fear; I must remove my shoes, the ground I stand on is holy. L: it is vanishing, flowing. A streaming world of being: God — EL. Thus, the mysteries taught the truth of the realities within sound, which we try to approximate today through 'speech formation' exercises. Through this threefold schooling, the mystery student of olden times mastered these three means of cognition: word, sign and handshake. In so far as one learnt to feel and grasp, one was able to differentiate things. If one had the signs, one knew how to imitate all the secrets of nature. In the word, one learnt to know the inner human being.

We are dealing here with a condition of consciousness belonging to a pre-intellectual culture when a person was still 'heart-man', not 'head-man'. The decisive soul qualities were heart qualities; the soul's centre of gravity was not yet in thinking. This type of consciousness was dimmed in the Middle Ages. However, the world historic storm only took place in the modern period, which transformed the heart-man into the head-man. The new spiritual structure of the consciousness soul came into being along with the middle classes.

Rudolf Steiner then went on to explain to the workmen that political movements and associations were connected to the old mystery knowledge. The Carbonari were an Italian secret society at the beginning of the nineteenth century, which fought for national liberation using Masonic forms and ideals. The French equivalent (Charbonnerie) arose after the revolution of July 1830. But Rudolf Steiner points to the racist, nationalist circles which used specific symbols on their posters: 'Two intertwined snakes or else, if you want, a wheel that then transforms itself into a swastika.' He then drew the symbol on the board and explained that the original swastika, as well as its later version, the 'hooked cross', is an ancient symbol still well-remembered by Asians. The symbol works much more deeply than any abstract teaching. It was well known from tradition that the ancients expressed their domination in such symbols. Through them, people were held together; community is founded in the magic of cultic fragments and ritual elements.

In his memoirs, Emil Leinhas[2] took down the following statement of Rudolf Steiner's: 'Those people who now bring the swastika to Central Europe know exactly what they are doing. It works.' And in 1920, when he heard about the right-wing Kapp Putsch,* he explained that the reign of criminals was beginning in Germany. Two years later, this criminal organization was to take aim at Rudolf Steiner.

From the above presentation we can make the following inferences. Signs or symbols (e.g. cross, circle, swastika, penta-gram, hexagram…) amalgamate meaning and image in an 'image of meaning'. They must be seen as pointers that are meant to direct our thoughts, our representations and our sensations in very specific directions. They originate in the mythical (i.e. the magic, cultic) epoch of mankind and work, even today, on the so-called subconscious. They cannot be fully explained because they are rooted more deeply in reality than our objective modern consciousness can reach. In the epoch of the mystery cultures, the deeper layers of the human soul were closer to the surface — as is still the case today in the small child, who cannot protect its consciousness from its surroundings.

Rites and cults were legitimate means for leadership of human beings who were still dependent, still embodied in the group soul. Today, these deeper layers of the soul have lost some of their significance for waking consciousness — but they are still there. Under specific conditions they can become intensely powerful both in positive and in negative ways. The psychologist Carl Jung has shown that the older, deeper layers of the soul can be activated through the performance of old rituals, even when under new guises.

The National Socialists mastered specific cultic-ritual methods with virtuosity. Among those were the cult of personality, or of

---

* An attempted coup in March 1920 against the Weimar Republic and German Revolution of 1918–19.

the leader (not a privilege reserved to their movement, as the Stalin era has shown). Among them, too, were the mass demonstrations with waving flags and sonorous music. Marching diverts and kills thinking; it extinguishes the personality. In this way the masses are prepared at the right moment to be reached by suggestive slogans. The blasphemous greeting 'Heil Hitler' also belongs here — blasphemous because one became the recipient of a greeting that had been reserved for God. All these cultic elements helped in building up power.

To those in the know, the use of the swastika showed what spirit had fathered National Socialism. The gesture backwards towards an ancient symbol spoke to 'old' layers of the soul. As soon as those were mobilized, a condition arose that was not adequate for modern consciousness, a condition which naturally had to work in unhealthy ways. From the very beginning National Socialism was never a form of progress, but was regression, reaction and anachronism. The negative, destructive forces which came to the fore through it made sensible the symbol that coincided with these forces. An article by Ernst Hagemann ('Der Nationalsozialismus', 1965) offers much interesting material, some of which I will present here.

In the summer of 1937 the House of German Art was dedicated in Munich. First there was a procession where a gigantic swastika surrounded by four eagles was paraded. The author explains: 'The renegade son of the Catholic Church had learnt enough in this respect about the methods preserved over centuries, and had no scruples in using what he had learnt for his own purposes.' Art, too, collaborated in 'raising the "mood barometer" of the masses. He wanted to smelt the heterogeneous elements of the masses into one with the help [of the arts]. All were to flow together in the great basin of homogeneity and form one single, blindly fanatical mass, ready to be led, ready to subject itself to its tamer, and to burst out in hysterical, ecstatic cries ... The Führer and his paladins revealed themselves as the celebrants of this celebration.' After sundown when darkness had fallen, light projectors lit up, forming a dome of light on the field. 'The assembly found itself surrounded by a wall of blood-red flags. On the Führer's platform flags were stretched Roman-style between the light-coloured travertine pillars, and the National Socialist emblem stood out from the white background. On such a stage is accomplished the ritualization of mass propaganda, which a satanic psychology uses for the enchantment of the masses.'

It is interesting to note here the parallels with some evangelist preachers who call themselves 'God's machine-gun' and who master the same technique of emotionally misleading and deluding the masses. These are but different versions of the same forces, which have suffered a defeat ... but have not been overcome.

Hagemann closes the chapter on the Führer ritual with the statement: 'The celebration of cultic festivals, which National Socialism developed to a high level of perfection, also included a "mystery" which expressed itself in the blood-red flag. Hannah Arendt[3] has compared this emblem to Lenin's mummified corpse in the Red Square mausoleum. By contrast with the Russian reliquary of Lenin, the portable mystery-emblem of National Socialism corresponds best to a party of movement, and to its impulse for transformation.'

These procedures illustrate what Rudolf Steiner expressed in his lecture in November 1917:[4] 'A certain tendency of mankind towards more occult principles will become strongly noticeable... Small groups of people will gain access to influence and gain great powers over others.' Furthermore, the background of the SS expedition to Tibet has become well known. As Rudolf Steiner explained to the Goetheanum workmen on 20 May 1924,[5] 'decadent Atlantean culture' has survived up till now in Tibet. There, it is still known that knowledge is power when it is kept secret. There they know how to lead people according to occult principles, i.e. the secret of the occult leadership which the German dictator sought for. Just as the Jesuits led the Indians of Paraguay, so the lamas led their faithful with old, even more powerful methods. This is clear from the impressive autobiography of the last Dalai Lama,[6] which describes the tragedy of Tibet since the Chinese conquest.

Let us mention here Steiner's sketch of 'The Druid Stone', which he painted in September 1923 after his visit to the Druid site at Penmaenmawr in Wales. On the left is a blue rock with the approximate outline of an old man sitting, hands clasped around his knees, looking over to his right. The entirety looks like an image of God as Nature would produce it. Behind the head of the old man are three altar-stones. By the central stone, the Druid stands completely upright, completely open to cosmic nature and sub-nature, and absorbed in the highest activity of earthly man — conscious interaction with the gods. On a projection of the blue rock, corresponding to the old man's knee, at the exact intersection of the diagonals of the picture, a second Druid is standing, but not bent over, by an isolated altar-stone. What the upper Druid took and brought down from the heavenly forces, the second Druid hands over to the uninitiated people of his community in the valley, to whom his eye, arm and body direction all point. On his altar is a symbol — the swastika. Nedella, the firm who printed the sketch following conversations with Steiner, says instead that it represents the sun and cosmic forces in the form of the four-petalled lotus flower. Through it we are pointed to the centre of strength and consciousness in the lower body of man. In older epochs the dark depths of life, of will and of sexuality were the gate of the spiritual world, the lower door which is now closed. Up till now, man has only conquered the head region, where sense and nerve processes are localized. Man is only totally master of himself in the light of thinking. This is why modern education is centred in this upper pole, whereas old schooling started at the lower pole, and was only possible under the strong direction of a guru. But in the lowest also resides the highest. Development only reaches its final goal when the last have become the first. The forces of the Holy Grail lead us further along this path and illuminate the darkness.

A glance at the past helps us to see what has happened. The hallowed symbol of Druidic old Europe, whose level corresponded to that of the third cultural epoch, has fallen into the hands of the opposing power, the adversary. He has taken over the symbol which now, in the fifth cultural epoch, releases forces

of destruction. Passion, violence and fear break out—the three
sinister companions arise.

Now we can ask the principal question which still remains to
be clarified. It comes out of the representation of the 'third
kingdom', which showed us the picture of the Medium posi-
tioned in the centre as a vacuum of hellish, suctional forces. In
which environment was the Medium prepared? Which force
fields come into play? Which powers use him?

Joachim Besser's 1950 article in *Die Pforte* ('The Prehistory of
National Socialism') gives us an initial orientation. The author
establishes that occultism stood as the godfather at the birth of
National Socialism, and then develops his theme as follows.
Occultism is the attempt to master life with occult means, to
push it further down into the realm of the mysterious through
the use of supersensible powers. This is a typically oriental
attitude and completely out of place in the West. Conse-
quently, theosophy with its Indo-Buddhist influences—and,
later, anthroposophy—are foreign bodies in the West. At core,
all occult teachings up till now have claimed that the only possible access to the deepest secrets is through special occult
teaching and initiation after a long period of schooling. Only a
very small circle of esotericists knows the secret; this circle is
appointed to lead the uninitiated. This teaching is an inheritance from a prehistory of magical thinking. In the nineteenth
century, under the influence of biological-naturalistic thinking,
racial theory was applied to historical writing. The pioneers in
this approach were the Frenchman Arthur de Gobineau with
his work *The Inequality of Human Races* (1855)[7] and the German-
by-choice Houston Stewart Chamberlain whose *The Foundations
of the Nineteenth Century* (1899) was Kaiser Wilhelm II's
favourite reading matter. All notable historians rejected the
'racial idea', in which history is determined solely by the iron
law of race, and the purity or degeneration of the races. In this
view the white race is the only one to create culture and
values. Within the white race Aryans are supposedly the most
valuable. Among them, in turn, are the Germans (being the
least racially mixed). According to Gobineau, the most obvious

opposite of the Germans are the Semites, who are bodily degenerate and spiritually uncreative.

At the turn of the nineteenth and twentieth centuries, the momentous connection of occultism and the 'racial idea' took place. From now on, the occult formula became as follows. Mankind comprises several races. But the only race that has the capacity to discover the secret of the world is the supersensibly gifted Aryo-German race. That is why it is appointed to take a leading role. All others are there to serve it — the master race.

The political consequences of this occult formula are easy to deduce. This is the foundation for any understanding of National Socialism. In a way, it is a joke of history that National Socialism, of occult origin, banned 'anthroposophic, theosophic and all other occult tendencies'.

In the second part of Joachim Besser's article, the author shows in which surroundings the Medium learnt the occult ground-formula in its racist translation. Those are familiar locations: pre-WWI Vienna, and Munich before — and especially after — World War I.

Let us look at pre-WWI Vienna first. In the lectures that were the basis for his book *The Life and Times of Rudolf Steiner*, Emil Bock described this milieu. Vienna, the imperial city of about two million people on the banks of the 'beautiful blue Danube', the capital city of a kind of super-Switzerland of thirteen national-ities, the city of music and of the refined enjoyment of life, described by Stefan Zweig as 'the town of yesterday' — this Vienna had an underground of 'spiritualist history' without parallel. There were vast numbers of secret societies and all kinds of remarkable ethnic-based and racist alliances and orders, whose furthest offshoots included political parties. Worthy of mention was the Pan-German Movement led by Georg Ritter von Schönerer, which demanded the attachment of Austria to the German Empire and represented an aggressive anti-Semitic nationalism. Then there was the Christian-Socialist Party of the Viennese Lord Mayor Karl Lueger, which steered a clerical, anti-Semitic and anti-Marxist course. In the background, the two most influential secret societies were the ones led by the macabre writer Guido von List and the equally secret Order of the New Templars led by a defrocked Cistercian monk by the name of Jörg Lanz von Liebenfels.

There is no doubt that Rudolf Steiner was aware of this 'underground'. List and Lanz were mentioned in a book he spent much time studying, *Vom Jenseits der Seele – die Geheimgesellschaften in kritischer Betrachtung* ('Beyond the Soul – A Critical Examination of Secret Societies') (1917), written by the Berlin professor of philosophy, Max Dessoir. In the chapter titled 'Occult Science', under the heading 'Theosophy', we find: (1) Race Mystique, represented by List and Lanz; (2) Christian Science; (3) Neo-Buddhism; and, (4) Anthroposophy. Before Steiner examined Dessoir's questionable methods in his *Riddles of the Soul* (CW 21), he attacked him in the cycle, *The Karma of Materialism* (CW 176). On that occasion, he specified what his relationship to List had been. It consisted in the fact that in the early 1880s he had received a publication by List, but had sent it back, finding it dilettantish and useless.

Guido von List, son of a rich Viennese merchant, lived from 1848 to 1919. At the age of 14 he made an unusual decision. In front of a ruined altar in a catacomb of St Stephen's Cathedral in Vienna, he pledged to build a temple to Wotan when he was older. His life's work was in the service of this resolve. He became a merchant, then secretary of the Austrian Alpine Society, whose members used the 'Heil' greeting. As a pioneer of the exploration of German antiquity and of its revival, he founded his own society, the Armanenschaft. He was joined there by theosophist Franz Hartmann and the Lord Mayor of Vienna, Lueger. According to List, the Armans were the initiates of an original Germanic cultural epoch and the leaders of the so-called Aryo-Germanic race. They were the sole possessors of the ability to know the world-secret. In this consists their godlike nature and their vocation to rule. Combined with radical anti-Semitism, this claim to rule was represented by the Society. The instrument of this rule of the Aryo-Germans was to be a state with an occult leadership consisting of a group of men, who were consecrated in priestly fashion. List thought of himself as the 'high Aryan leader', who had the key to Germanic runic wisdom and who recognized the swastika as the highest secret sign of the Armans. He describes the swastika as 'the demonic fire of revolt that with volcanic strength breaks the fetters, when obstacles attempt to stop the germination of new ideas'. List was a prolific writer. According to Lanz, he had the effect of a 'psychological medium' and always found rich patrons to finance his enterprise.

Equally lucky was the even more suspect Lanz, who called himself Jörg Lanz von Liebenfels. He was a teacher's son from Vienna. Born in 1874, he died in 1954. He is said to have changed the date and place of his birth to mislead astrologers. His childhood wish was to become a Templar Knight and to own castles or to rebuild them. His strongest impression in youth was Marschner's opera *The Templar Knight and the Jewess*, which delighted him to ecstasy. In 1893, at age 19, he entered the Cistercian abbey of Heiligenkreuz, which has played an important role in Austrian history. The following year he wrote a piece about a grave which had been dug up in the cloister of the abbey. The find held great significance for him. A stone carving showed a manly figure stepping with bare feet over a man-beast. It became the symbol of his ideology. He saw in the relief the triumph of the higher race over the lower races. In 1899 he left the abbey, officially for 'carnal love'. The priest and runaway monk now declared himself Baron von Liebenfels and in 1900 founded the New Templar Order, Ordo Novi Templi, which is still in existence.

The Templar Order, a name which Lanz usurped, thus called itself after Solomon's temple in Jerusalem, where originally the Grand Master of the Templars resided. The tragic story of the fall of the Templars is well known. The Master of the Order, Jacques de Molay, and 54 knights were burned at the stake after a show trial set up by King Philip IV of France, whose motivation was to fabricate grounds for confiscating the treasure of the Order. Lanz's foundation was meant to be a reminder of the intentions of this most important of the religious knightly orders. He provided his secret society (organized on the model of the Catholic orders) with texts: a scripture of 'all Aryan heroic peoples'; a breviary (which contemporary members still pray to); an exhaustive Bible commentary; and, a translation of the Psalms. There were also cultic, so-called Grail Festivals. Only blond, blue-eyed men devoted to the purity of the race were allowed into the order. According to Lanz's theory, civilization would only survive through the 'planned breeding of people of Aryan race, bearers of the state and culture'. This, of course, means nothing other than race war under the sign of the swastika – or, as the slogan went, 'Racial struggle including the castrating knife'.

Lanz founded not only a 'religion of the cult of the race' for the Aryan master race, he also delivered the matching picture of world development, which goes more or less as follows. In the race-pure Paradise, the Fall took the form of miscegenation, through the alliance of the Aryo-heroic people with the 'dark races', the result of demonic bungling. In order to free the Aryan race from original sin, from 'sodomy', the hero Jesus Frauja appears (Lanz prefers to use the Gothic name from the Ulfilas Bible) and gives the commandment 'Love your kind as yourself'. According to Lanz, the Catholic Church of the Middle Ages became a kind of 'Institute for race breeding'. But decay would proceed until such time as the blond race achieved world rule over the inferior races. Its prophet is Lanz and its executor is the Medium. Lanz named this nonsense Ariosophy and spread it through his *Ostara* bulletin, which reached a print run of 10,000 copies. Hitler was among its readers; he visited Lanz in 1909 and obtained some back issues. After the First World War the bulletin changed its format – it never lacked patrons or subscribers – but had to stop publication after the annexation of Austria. Its production was no longer opportune.

In a letter from 1932, Lanz shows how he sees the political developments, and what meaning he attributes to his own work: 'Do you know that Hitler is one of our students? You will see that he, and through him we ourselves, will vanquish, and a movement will be stirred that will set the whole world trembling.' In National Socialism and Fascism, in the Spanish and Hungarian dictatorships, and in the American Ku-Klux-Klan, Lanz saw the beginnings of a new development. In his opinion, the strongest force in this Fascist International was the 'German Swastika movement directly derived from Ariosophy'.

No doubt there were connections between Lanz and the Medium. But it would be naive to try and 'explain' the entire German development since 1933 from these facts, as was the case in an article by Wilfried Daim, who published his research on Lanz under the title *Der Mann, der Hitler die Ideen gab* ('The man who gave Hitler his ideas').

This glance at the 'spiritual' underground in Vienna may be sufficient. Let us now leave the city and visit Munich. Here the Medium appears in 1913, and stays there until the outbreak of war. There then follow the years at the Western Front, and at the end of the war his poisoning by nerve gas. The latter led to temporary blindness and affected his processes of elimination, which allowed ahrimanic forces to take over. (For comparison purposes, see Rudolf Steiner's account, 29 November 1919, of Ludendorff's situation during the storming of Liège.)[8] At the end of 1918, the Medium is a changed man, more determined upon political activity, and returns to Munich.

The atmosphere in Munich has been well characterized by Ludwig Klages. He stresses the 'primitive sensual joy with its healthy freedom of morals', the 'readiness to hold celebrations', the 'splendiferous processions and religious services drowning in the smoke of incense', and 'the characteristic aptitude for a kind of mass intoxication during Carnival, May celebrations and Oktoberfest'. Around the year 1900, the Munich borough of Schwabing was a bohemian centre surpassing Berlin in the 1920s in its provocative rejection of middle class values. Intellectuals, cranks, artists, those with wrecked lives, all meet in clubs, at studio parties, and participate in nightlong discussions. The most prominent among those groups was the circle of the 'Cosmic-types' (*Kosmiker*): the mythologist Schüler, the psychologist Klages, and the man of letters, Wolfskehl. Stefan George was also part of their gatherings when he was in Munich.

Alfred Schüler offers something of interest for our discussion, for he was the source of impulses which influenced the Medium. His lectures were held as late as 1922 in the Bruckmann Salon, where the Medium also surfaced. Klages, who was his acquaintance, published his lectures in 1940 and added a description of his life. Also illustrative is a characterization of Schüler in the memoirs of the archaeologist Ludwig Curtius.

Schüler came from Mainz, where he was born in 1865, and was the son of a Catholic lawyer. He grew up in Zweibrücken and studied law, archaeology and history of art in Munich, but never received a degree. A dissertation on the swastika, planned in 1895, was never finished. He broke up with George over his anti-Semitism. One may note his relationship with the Empress Elisabeth, whom he hoped to gain as a student, and to the ailing Nietzsche, whom he wanted to cure with the performance of wild and frenzied dances. (The plan never materialized because he was too poor to afford the necessary copper panoply.) His lectures were tricked out of him by Klages, who got him to speak by asking leading questions and then had them secretly written down. He died in 1932 and was buried in his Roman toga — he thought himself to be a Roman of Nero's time.

Klages declared Schüler to have been 'by far the most knowledgeable about the secrets of antiquity'. Even as a boy he kept looking for ancient shards and fragments. When he held them in his hand and inhaled their 'fluid', their 'biotic sediment', as he called it, he would come under a kind of intoxicating spell in which he would embark on visionary descriptions of the sunken culture. This atavistic gift explains Schüler's opinion that the actual insights into the being of the world and of life are not the result of any logical-discursive science but of an inner vision or, in his words, 'not cerebral idling' but 'a blood-beacon'. This, however, is a form of cognition belonging to pre-intellectual cultures, the dull clairvoyance of a humanity still caught in the group soul. The relations of this stage of development he called 'the open life' — the time 'when the feeling of at-oneness with the unbounded universe' still reigned. Then came the process of 'falling away from the light (un-lighting)'. The 'all-unifying etheric clothing', the 'eternal city', the 'etheric unity', disappeared. A long stretch of darkness and emptiness, cold and suffering must be travelled. 'Moloch's Christianity, spiritually related to Judaism, has stifled life', for it devours the youthful cosmic forces, just as the Babylonian god Moloch devoured the children brought to him as sacrifices. 'The weasel Judah sneaked into the heart of life. For two thousand years it destroyed the warm, throbbing, dreaming, sparkling mother-heart.' But there is hope that a new world will arise in the present, and that life will once again become 'open' as a result of the conscious communion with the secret of the blood. The reign of a youth under the sign of Eros is about to begin, and salvation will appear in the symbol of the swastika. For the swastika is the counter-symbol of the martyr's cross of the Christian. This is the language of Schüler. Many of his proverb-like sayings sound like prophecies. 'We will throw fire into the night, and incandescent copper, and it will boil in city and village and charcoal kiln, down to the last poplar-blackened cottage roof...' And, 'Murder the Father, before he devours your child, your soul, and release the ancient coil, the hundred-spoked wheel of fire. Hell, the heart of Gaia, will help you.' This should be enough to indicate what is at stake here. But we are still in the vestibule. Those named so far, List, Lanz and Schüler, can just be taken for lunatics in their own right; those who are to come now have other backgrounds. We now touch the border zone of real occult societies.

At this point some remarks are in order. Rudolf Steiner explained the methods and goals of the occult societies particularly during the Great War. Occult power over groups of people is striven for in those circles. The concept of occultism must be understood in a fairly general way. Anything comes under the heading of occultism as long as it removes itself from knowledge. For instance, this would also be the case with nuclear physics. One can also speak of occult influences in some forms of modern advertising. Through the conscious 'reaching into the subconscious' one attempts to harness people for goals that they either do not want, or do not know. Normal waking consciousness is circumvented. One penetrates into the soul through the back door, as it were, in order to exert the desired influence there.

As for the students of actual occult societies, they first must submit themselves to a specific soul-training. In particular, they are expected to immerse themselves in specific images for such a length of time that the latter rise 'plastically' in front of their inner eye, and appear to be external sensations. The images become autonomous, but the student is never allowed to lose control over the 'realities' created by him. Further intimate proceedings enable the student to influence other people, to imbue them with their thoughts, and to implant perceptions in others without their becoming aware of it. The goal of such schooling is to direct human beings like marionettes, through occult measures which are inaccessible to the control of the ego, in order to succeed in remotely controlling the soul.

It is easy to understand that the gifted candidate, who described himself as the 'drummer' or 'the nameless lance-corporal', was the perfect object for occult influence.

Let us look further at the figures in the Munich milieu.

First, there is the so-called Baron Rudolf von Sebottendorf, who also went by another alias, Erwin Torre. In reality he was Rudolf Glauer, born in Saxony in 1875. He emigrated to Turkey before the First World War, adopted the name Sebottendorf and played a leading role in the Balkan War of 1912–13 in the Turkish movement of the Red Crescent. After acquiring an education in Turkey—thanks to a Jewish merchant—and having become a member of the Rosicrucian Order (a Freemasonic and Theosophic secret society), he appeared in Germany in 1917, quite well furnished financially, and then established contacts with Masonic 'brothers' and other similar societies. By 1917 the representatives of these lodges had admitted that Germany had lost the war, whereupon they started making preparations for the 'national rebirth'. The German Empire was divided into provinces, and Sebottendorf was allocated Bavaria. He established his quarters in Munich and founded the Thule Society, a racist Masonic lodge which had an exoteric periphery and an esoteric core. The unimportant members of this Order worked in the foreground, while the ones who pulled the strings remained out of sight. (The name Thule refers to Ultima Thule, a remote island which had been spared conquest by the Roman Church and had preserved the ruins of old Germanic wisdom in the songs of the *Edda*.) During the Bavarian Soviet Republic in post-war Munich, the Thule Society became active and organized political terror against the Eisner government. There is no doubt that these circles were responsible for the attempt on Rudolf Steiner's life in 1922.

Historical research is aware of the Thule Society, and it knows of Sebottendorf and his 1933 book *Bevor Hitler kam* ('Before Hitler Came'), which promised 'Original information about the early history of the National Socialist movement'. The author points out that the Thule Society brought about the astonishing ascent and the political breakthrough of the Medium, thanks to its helpers and the means at its disposal. Sebottendorf claims responsibility for having forged 'the Führer's armour'.

All this is well known, as are also the slanders against Rudolf Steiner contained in Sebottendorf's book. Less well known is his background. An autobiographical novel *Der Talisman des Rosenkreuzers* ('The Talisman of the Rosicrucian') of 1925 gives indications about his schooling and also contains a remark about his encounter with anthroposophy. The decisive clue is in his work *Die Praxis der alten türkischen Freimauerei: Der Schlüssel zum Verständnis der Alchimie* ('The Practice of the old Turkish Free-masonry — The Key to the Understanding of Alchemy'), which was reprinted in 1954. In it Sebottendorf explains: 'Modern Freemasonry is — and is not — the continuation of medieval Freemasonry. It is in its external forms; however, when it comes to the teaching method and to its substance, it has totally abandoned the ways of the old Freemasonry.' Namely, it no longer has any system of exercises of the kind Sebottendorf had received from the Bektashi Dervish order. A canon of exercises of this kind was known in Europe in 1913 through a secretary at the Turkish Legation in Bern, who had openly been sent by his superiors in the order. At that time, the oriental method began to infiltrate Europe. It provided for a forced training of the will, a kind of anti-eurythmy with I–A–O exercises and a threefold schooling in 'sign, feeling and sound', all of it connected with astrological aspects. One may contrast this with the schooling method out of the pole of consciousness, as Rudolf Steiner presented it in his writings. The latter takes the opposite route. It goes 'from top to bottom', is completed under the control of the ego, and gradually moves consciousness from the centre to the periphery. The difference with oriental praxis is obvious.

Let us go one step further. Lurking in the background of the Order of Thule we find the very opaque Karl Haushofer, founder of geopolitical studies (geopolitics) in Germany. Born in 1869 to a professorial family in Munich, he decided to follow a military career and graduated from the military academy with high honours. At that point he embarked on a prolonged trip to Asia, and acquired a thorough knowledge of Japan as well as of the Japanese language. Many years later Japan was opened to his son Albrecht; like his father, he learned to know Japan from the inside. Haushofer took part in the First World War as a Bavarian Major General, after which he received a professorship in Munich. His assistant Rudolf Hess made contact with the Medium, so that Haushofer visited them both during their imprisonment in Landsberg Prison, following the failure of the 1923 Putsch. After this we have a gap. In later years, he had differences with his conversation partners in Landsberg. In 1946 Haushofer killed his wife, then took his own life according to Japanese ritual.

The background of this life is hinted at by his son Albrecht Haushofer in one of the 'Moabit Sonnets', which were written shortly before his murder by the SS.

The Father
A deep fairy tale from the Orient
tells us that spirits of evil force
sit as prisoners in the night of the sea,
locked up by God's apprehensive hand

Until, once in a millennium, luck
grants one fisherman the decision
that can free the bound ones,
if he doesn't throw the find back into water.

[Every 1000 years the doors of hell are unlocked.]

For my father, fate had spoken.
It lay once in his power
to push the demon back into the jail.

My father broke the seal.
The breath of evil he did not see.
He let the demon disperse into the world.

An elucidating remark by the father belongs alongside this poem. On the first day of the Polish campaign, Hess remarked to Haushofer that the war would soon be over. This was the same illusion people had in 1914 ('when the leaves fall, we will be back home'), to which Haushofer answered, 'Don't forget! When you sit on a tiger, you can't jump off'.[9] The question arises: who trained the rider so that he was able to jump on the back of a tiger? Haushofer did his part. In the background to these events worked the influence of a man who, among those described in this chapter, is both the most important and also the most difficult to see through: the 'Master' Gurdjieff, born in Armenia, who came to be an opponent of Rudolf Steiner.

The following book helps to orientate us; it is by a former student of Gurdjieff's, the French writer Louis Pauwels, written in collaboration with Jacques Bergier: *The Morning of the Magicians* (1963). Aside from that, Oluf Falck-Ytter has written about these complex issues in the magazine *Christengemeinschaft* (May 1959).

Gurdjieff himself has written quite a few volumes, one of which includes a derogatory remark about Rudolf Steiner. This personality can only be grasped in the reflections of its manifold effects. Here are the most important details in his life story, in so far as it is known. George Ivanovich Gurdjieff was born around 1870 in Alexandropol, which today is in the republic of Armenia. The son of an Armenian mother and a Greek father, he pursued various academic studies and attended the seminary in Tbilisi (like his compatriot Stalin*). He subsequently travelled in Asia for several years. On his return to Europe he visited its principal

*Stalin was from Georgia, born in Gori in Tbilisi.

cities. He then founded schools—which he called 'Institutes for the Harmonious Development of Man'—first in Georgia, then in France and the USA. The one in Fontainebleau became the best known—it was founded in 1922. In Paris and New York he gave public demonstrations of 'movement exercises' with his students, directed by him. Later he renounced such public performances and devoted himself to smaller groups of students. He died in 1949 at the American Hospital in Neuilly. But his effect went further. A succession of students spread his teachings in Western thought forms. The best known of those was P. D. Ouspensky, who died in 1947 at the end of the Second World War.

Gurdjieff's intentions belong to a development which started in the nineteenth century. Since then, there has been a noticeable advance of oriental schoolings. These aim at the systematic dissolution of modern consciousness, at the unsettling of the Central European spirit. Gurdjieff's exercises were aimed at tearing man out of the connectedness of thinking. They effected a development of the will which escapes from the control of the ego, and are in their essence completely unchristian. Looking back to his time as a student, Pauwels says it clearly: 'We were, to be precise, dehumanized', and again, 'At the time when I was a disciple of the philosopher Gurdjieff, I never heard one word: the word "love".'

Let us sum things up. We have observed the eruption of decadent Asiatic spirituality in Europe in the form of magical and astrological practices. The channels are: Sebottendorf and those behind him, Haushofer and the Order of Thule, Gurdjieff and his entourage. Their effects upon the Medium are actual, although difficult to prove, as the occult backgrounds are only rarely revealed by the light. But this much can be said: the 'knowers' of this movement were seeking a way to the source that gives power over other people. They wanted to follow a path that would enable them to rule the world, and they walked the path of power, as taught in their orders. They reached back into the past for the swastika, the sign of a magical cultural stage, and they unleashed destructive forces of will.

In 1907, in the course of a cultic Grail Festival, Lanz hoisted the first swastika flag at his 'Grail Castle', the ruin of Werfenstein on the Danube. It took place under the sign of racial war. That same year, Rudolf Steiner appeared publicly for the first time as an artist, designing the images of occult seals and the capitals of columns for the Munich Congress (which was also attended by Annie Besant, the president of the Theosophical Society). The seven seals show the astral archetypes of human development, which are also found in St John's Apocalypse. In part, Rudolf Steiner took over their forms from tradition, which he duly noted. But one seal was made anew – the seventh seal, which contains the 'universal meaning of human development', the reproduction of the mystery of the Holy Grail.

Let us bring to mind the Grail seal that Steiner gave to students of modern spiritual science as the new 'sign' for contemplative meditation – the transparent crystal cube, the image of the spatial world, still untouched by physical beings and events. Snakes representing the lower forces in man rise in three dimensions on the cube. They engender a purified higher nature, represented in the world-spirals. As the spiritual forces grow upwards, man becomes the chalice of the Holy Grail for the cosmic powers. They approach it in the form of a dove, the Holy Spirit, and find their likeness in the surrounding rainbow. The whole is surrounded by the ten letters of the Rosicrucian formula, which contains the law of the Holy Trinity.

The seals and capitals of the columns were intended for the Johannesbau ('John's Building'), which was intended to be built in Munich for the presentation of the Mystery Dramas. But the construction was prevented by local opposition, and Rudolf Steiner decided to move to the Dornach hill. On his way to Dornach for the laying of the foundation stone, he said (according to Karl Heyer), 'Now we go into exile.' Did he mean by this that Switzerland was distant from the flow of great events? 'In Munich there arose a spiritual vacuum, and this attracted, as it is wont to do, something else, something opposite ... and the anti-Goetheanum was erected there' – the Brown House. Thus writes Heyer in his autobiographical sketch. The events speak an unmistakeable language. The Gospel would have gone out from St John's building in Munich. From the Brown House of the counter-movement, the gospel of 'Blood and Soil' went out. German youth followed the latter. Rudolf Steiner, who saw through these developments, said in 1924 that the Youth Section in Dornach should be a kind of counter-stream to the racist forces, to the Freemasons with their orders, which were being put at the disposal of nationalist aspirations and were exerting a suggestive power over the young.

German development has shown how important the foundation of the Youth Section has been. Actually — and herein lies the tragedy — the hoped-for effect did not take place. The Pied Piper arrived and played the tune, which he himself had not composed. Many followed and were fascinated by it, misunderstanding their own aspirations. They were seeking a new orientation, but they came to a momentously wrong decision and mistook the dragon for the spirit of the times, Michael.

3. Klingsor

Now we can provisionally sum up this presentation of the historical reality of the year 1933. This means looking back to the previous chapter. The plan and the framework must be visible before we can erect a roof over the edifice.

The first argument had to do with the time frame of the phenomenon that goes by the name of National Socialism. In 1933 a commendable book appeared that was intended by its author, Roman Boos, to be a contribution to the events of his time: *Rudolf Steiner während des Weltkrieges* ('Rudolf Steiner During the World War'). It establishes that since 1933 there had arisen in Germany a strong will and, 'no matter how one sees the exterior form in which this will lives, it is the clear duty of the non-Pharisee to look for its human core'. Here lies a tragic mistake: this will had no human core, no ego-substance. On the contrary, there was nothing but a spiritual vacuum. The mover of the developments that started in 1933 with implacable dynamism was himself led; he was a Medium.

From this insight there followed a second argument, which attempted to answer the question: In which milieu was the Medium prepared? The process of 'construction' goes through three stages: pre-war Vienna, pre-war Munich and post-war Munich. Between the second and third stages lie proceedings which can only be fully explained through the kind of 'historio-psychopathology' which Rudolf Steiner had called for, a science of the illness of the soul with a focus on history.[1] I have in mind here the events which can be identified as repression of the ego and the eruption of the 'demonic', so that the man who had been a failure in school as well as in his profession was able to become the master of total annihilation. He started out without any concrete skill and was only provided with a gift—a virtuoso technique of human manipulation. He emerged like a ghost out of the phantom world of the Weimar Republic and ended in a similar vein, leaving behind him a world in ruin and a blood guilt without precedent.

The whole monstrosity was set in train by pseudo-cultic methods under the sign of the swastika. Through such practices, 'old' layers of consciousness covered by the waking consciousness were activated. As a result, its adherents experienced factual alterations of consciousness, which depth-psychology diagnosed as 'mass delirium', as epidemic illness. In the summer of 1964 the Stuttgart working group 'Arzt und Seelsorger' ('Doctor and Pastor') studied this complex and published the proceedings of its conference under the title 'Mass insanity in history and in the present'.[2] The psychologist Carl Jung claimed to recognize in National Socialism the 'Wotan' archetype.[3] According to Jung, soul dispositions pass down from generation to generation in the form of archetypes (i.e. primitive forms or images) which keep producing the same ideas and representations. The archetypal Wotan is the Germanic god of storm and drunkenness, which through Christianity has been transformed into the devil. As a 'supremely powerful magician', he would have thus seized part of the German folk and have become the liberator of passions and aggressions. How different this is from the Wotan described by Rudolf Steiner to the Wandervögel[*] of Koberwitz, a Wotan walking in the elements! Thus there took place a collective pathological phenomenon, the 'St Vitus dance of the twentieth century', which from a psychological point of view is connected with the loss of symbolism, the general foundering of values, and a religious vacuum into which deluded notions of salvation have made their way.

Such an interpretation misreads reality, for it sees the spiritual merely as a projection at the soul level, not as an autonomous realm of beings active in manifold layers. The cognitive assumption of anthroposophy is ignored: that human beings can find access to the sphere of objective spirituality, when they train

---

[*]The popular movement of German youth groups, founded initially in 1896, with the goal of shaking off society's restrictions and getting back to nature and freedom.

their consciousness to the higher levels of Imagination, Inspiration and Intuition.

Having rejected as insufficient the interpretation offered by depth-psychology, we can ask the basic question of this entire research: Which spiritual powers were using the actors of 1933 for their own purposes? Which forces were acting in the spiritual world behind the stage of outer events? It is a question of 'transcendent powers' which, for instance, Alfred Weber recognizes even though—as an agnostic—he denies that they can be known.[4] Over the heads of their contemporaries a higher history is being played out. Earthly history is but the shadow cast by this 'supra-history'. This is why, nowadays, we must create concepts which make the interplay of supersensible forces and of historically 'graspable' events understandable for us. This is the specific task of an anthroposophical view of history which begins to penetrate to the level of knowledge commensurate with the twentieth century.

Let us look once again at the phenomenon, which we seek to grasp with the sense of a perceptive power of judgement. I refer to the complex of facts described by Hannah Arendt in her book *Eichmann in Jerusalem*.[5] The notorious criminal is insignificant as a person, but the investigation reveals a psychology of evil, which is what concerns us here. The book's shocking subtitle, *A Report on the Banality of Evil*, does not mean that evil is rendered harmless, but points to an epidemic of illness caused by the virus of evil infiltrating the whole national body. This illness led to a system of totalitarian rule which planned and carried out genocide. Evil became banal, a daily occurrence. As a result certain karmic consequences followed— karmic consequences between Germans and Jews, whose world-historical dimensions are only beginning to dawn on our awareness. The question comes up again: Who is the actual originator, the true driving force of this monstrous event? Who, in the end, has the responsibility for what was committed in the name of the Germans?

We must look at the underlings. First of all Adolf Eichmann, and only the essentials need be reported. He was born in 1906, the son of an accountant in Solingen, and was unsuccessful both

in high school and at the polytechnic. His self-declared profession was mechanical engineer, which he practised in various
firms in Austria. He was a member of several associations in his
youth: the Young Men's Christian Association, the Wandervögel,
and others. While attempting to join the Masonic lodge Schlar-
affia, he was invited to join the SS and became a member of the
Nazi Party and SS in 1932. After completing his SS training, he
was assigned the task of reporting on the Jewish Question for the
security services. Here, as Hannah Arendt points out, he became
a specialist on the 'Jewish Question'. During the final days of the
war, he bragged to relatives, 'I will gladly jump into my grave,
for the awareness that I have five million Jews [he always called
them enemies of the Reich] on my conscience gives me a great
sense of satisfaction.'

The implementer of the so-called Final Solution, the physical
destruction of Jewry, was able to go underground after the war.
In 1950, he is smuggled through Austria and Italy by a secret SS
organization and equipped with a refugee's passport in the name
of Ricardo Klement. He goes to Argentina, becomes an employee
in the Buenos Aires Mercedes plant, sends for his family and
manages to live in the local Nazi colony. Then he gets tired of
being 'an anonymous wanderer between worlds'. His big-
headedness and craving for status, confirmed by all witnesses,
together with his ludicrous *petit bourgeois* ways, lead to a famous
interview, which is publicized in Germany and later in the USA.
Despite this, it takes the Israeli secret service years to ascertain
the true identity of Ricardo Klement. His capture and kidnap-
ping follow in 1960, and after a trial in Jerusalem, his execution in
1962.

What do these facts show? Let us limit ourselves to one single
fact: the weak ego, which expresses itself in bragging and a greed
for authority. Among many self-descriptions, the following
unmasks him best. After the command structure breaks down,
on the day of capitulation he notes that 'from now on [he] would
have to lead a difficult, leaderless life', that he 'can't turn anywhere to get directions', and that 'there is no way to obtain
orders and instructions from anywhere, no relevant regulations

on which to draw', in short that 'a totally unknown life opens up'. A difficult, leaderless life was not his thing. In his heart, he had made room for a higher one whose directions he followed without asking for justifications — an egoless man, an empty shell, the instrument of radical evil.

Through the psyche of this non-man, we can look into the inner soul of his 'Leader'. This was the same *petit-bourgeois* character and egolessness, the same puppet-like functioning. Only, the Leader himself had made room in his own heart for an even 'higher' one, who ruled him as the opponent of the German folk-spirit.

At this point our interpretation requires that we refer to anthroposophical knowledge with respect to a 'second original Fall'. This historically observable event emancipates one's thinking from the supporting moral forces, erodes one's sense of responsibility and autonomy to make individual decisions. While the first, luciferic Fall gave humanity the knowledge of good and evil ('you shall be as gods knowing good from evil'), the second, ahrimanic Fall veils such knowledge and causes moral blindness, which was described by Steiner as 'moral insanity': you will be like beasts, not knowing good from evil.

Bruno Bettelheim (*The Informed Heart*, London 1960) and Raul Hilberg (*The Destruction of the European Jews*, Chicago 1961) have documented historically this tragic development. Simplified, their conclusions are as follows. In the totalitarian system, the human being becomes a totally controllable 'animal-like species', a 'living corpse', an 'indoctrinated robot'. The totalitarian State is an organization of depersonalized, egoless managers, and millions of dehumanized slaves who represent nothing but the 'incarnation of evil'.

Many contemporaries have said it ... some out of intuition, others out of a deeper knowledge. The animal in man is in charge, the animal principle, the animal as the symbol for cognition which has been misled. We have already spoken about it, the Beast mentioned in the Apocalypse. It rises out of the earth in the form of an animal, 'which has two horns, looks like a lamb but speaks like a dragon'. The most important disclosures about this enemy of mankind are found in the *De Occulta Philosophia* of Agrippa of Nettesheim, and in Rudolf Steiner on the subjects of black and white magic in the *Apocalypse of St John* (1908, CW 104), and in his historical reflections in *Three Streams in the Evolution of Mankind* (CW 184).[6]

According to tradition, the beast is Sorat. He is the Sun Demon, the enemy of the Lamb. Steiner has unveiled his historical influences and effects and his rhythm: 666 + 666 + 666. Sorat's attacks achieve success in the seventh, fourteenth and twentieth centuries.

Sorat, the leading ahrimanic spirit, was first active as the inspirer of the Academy at Gondishapur; 666 was the cosmic deadline for his effect. His plan had been to bring about a powerfully premature ripening of history within 2000 years, the duration of one whole cultural epoch. Before mankind had reached maturity, their still dreamy souls were to be confronted with the results of modern intellectualism, corresponding more or less to our current evolutionary stage. Every teacher knows the dangers of precocity, its poisoning effect on the souls of children and young people. If the Gondishapur impulse had been allowed to develop fully — it was stopped by Islam — humanity would not have reached its evolutionary goal; it would not have completed the formation of its sevenfold substance. Sorat's second attack led to the annihilation of the Knights Templar by Philip IV of France.

What happened at the onset of the twelve years of Nazi rule[7] has been graphically described by Karl Heyer: 'It was as if a dark, heavy wall of cloud were rising threateningly on the horizon, while the sun was still shining. Now it has almost reached the sun. Now it destroys it. Darkness spreads everywhere.' This description was based on an exact indication by Steiner, which Heyer repeated in his autobiographical sketch. In 1933 a dark, spiritual force, describable as the Sun Demon, would be revealed in social life. For those in the know, this prophecy was the key to understanding National Socialism. Steiner explained further that in 1933 a cosmic catastrophe would threaten, but would be diverted. Instead, a human catastrophe took place whose consequences cannot be predicted.

But let us remember what happened. In 1933, in the name of German culture, a programme of anti-humanism in the West and the destruction of European Jews was put into effect. Thus, the Germans distinguished themselves as a criminal nation unlike any other nation on earth — the Germans, in whose language the anthroposophical message was delivered. The 'Sorat-effect' in the social sphere came in through the state, which had become the instrument of evil through the totalitarian system of ego-less managers and their dehumanized slaves, through the power apparatus by which the 'animal species of man' has come to power.

But the Sorat element can only be active if human beings give him entry into history. The Führer (the led Leader) is the Medium.

Rudolf Steiner talked repeatedly about mediumship and the nature of a mediumistic being. For our purposes, the decisive indications are in the lecture cycle *True and False Paths in Spiritual Investigation* (CW 243). In the Medium, the parts of the brain which serve the ego are developed in such a way that they can be disconnected from the whole organism; thus, they no longer function at the disposal of the ego. Mediumistic consciousness and sleeping consciousness are polar opposites. In sleep man lives in his astral body and his ego. But in the medium's consciousness both ego and astral body are emptied. There thus arises a vacuum, and alien spiritual forces are able to attack. It is primarily the ahrimanic forces which 'have the appetite to replace the ego in the brain... This is the real mystery of mediumistic being: the possession by specific beings... Ahrimanic beings are present in the world with an intelligence far superior to man's intelligence... They are real supermen in their intelligence.' And for those in his audience who had not realized just how concrete such cognitions are, Rudolf Steiner added still more: 'Somnambulists (who are natural mediums) go around, whether they are venerated as mediums or whether they construct pure theories of the State, as in Bolshevism, or realize, like mediums, all kinds of things in the world; they go around in the present world and have no notion of the spiritual world.' If you replace the word Bolshevism by National Socialism (for they were truly brother enemies) and recall that Braunau was a centre of medium power, it will be clear that the 'led Leader' was a medium possessed by Ahriman.

Now to the theme regarding Klingsor. The last chapter closed with a reference to the Seventh Seal of the Apocalypse which reproduces the mystery of the Holy Grail. In Rudolf Steiner's *Occult Science* (CW 13), the knowledge of the 'new consecration with the Christ Mystery at its centre' is described as the 'wisdom of the Grail' and the new initiates are called 'Grail initiates'. Klingsor is the enemy of the Grail, and whoever speaks of Klingsor forces speaks of the counter-stream of anthroposophy, the counter-stream to the new initiation. According to Steiner, Klingsor represents the 'unchristian cosmology'.[8] Christian cosmology was originally founded on occult science. Just as the physical world revolves around the physical sun, so the super-sensible cosmos revolves around the Christ-Sun. Here lies the main difference between Steiner's occult science and the still unchristian occult teaching of Blavatsky.

We will only get hold of the difficult Klingsor theme if we try to grasp the figure of Klingsor as it appears in the poems and legends of the Middle Ages. Richard Wagner received his inspiration from these sources. His intuitive eye unlocked the substance of Klingsor's greatness, which he portrayed in *Parsifal*. There, Klingsor appears as the master of the enchanted castle in whose wondrous gardens he wrests the holy spear from an ailing Amfortas. Here we will draw upon the principal descriptions from the Middle Ages: Wolfram's *Parzival* and the troubadour poem 'The Minstrels' Contest at the Wartburg', which was composed *c.* 1260, half a century after *Parzival*.[9]

Wolfram recounts that Klingsor built the magic castle of *Chastelmerveil* (Montserrat) and held many souls captive there. His duchy is called Terra de Labur (Land of Toil), his capital city Capua. Klingsor is a renowned fighter but falls into ignominy when he abducts Iblis, the Queen of Sicily. Iblis's husband surprises the two of them in his castle of Kalot-Enbolot (Italian Caltabellotta) and 'in one cut makes Klingsor a capon'. Since then the castrated Klingsor has been following both men and women with burning hatred, especially those who still follow the rules of propriety. His greatest pleasure is to be able to deprive them of their joy.

Wolfram describes the disposition of soul of a black magician who has followed the requisite schooling. The first prerequisite is the forced renunciation of sexual love. Unnatural asceticism, unexpressed, repressed carnality has a way of turning into hatred of mankind. The first step is the destruction of the joy of others. The next step is instruction in magic arts and magic words, which Klingsor obtains in the town of Persida. It gives him power over all spirits, both good and evil, except for those under God's special protection.

The next source, 'The Minstrels' Contest at the Wartburg', includes in its second part a riddling contest between Klingsor, with his magic knowledge, and the pious Wolfram. Heinrich von Ofterdingen has called the most famous singers of the day to a competition, and has offered his own head as the prize. All are assembled in the Knights' Hall of Count Hermann von Thüringen. As the contest turns against Heinrich, the countess pleads for his life. But the poet, in distress, turns to his master Klingsor. The 'Master Cleric' of Hungary appears in the guise of a grocer who sells riddles instead of the usual wares. Now the contest between Klingsor and Wolfram begins. Wolfram manages to solve Klingsor's riddle, which had to do with Christian truths and mystical secrets. When he comes to the tenth and last riddle, Klingsor sends in the devil Nasion with the hardest astronomical questions. The expected result is that Wolfram, being a layman in star wisdom, will have to give up. Wolfram, however, sees through the devil's work. He calls upon God and the Virgin Mary, and at the sign of the cross the devilish magic must give way.

Taken all together, the various sources provide the following. Klingsor, who as a magician tried to fight the Holy Grail, was initiated in the black arts. His knowledge had been gleaned in Paris, while he later studied alchemy and astrology in Baghdad and Babylon. He is called the 'Master Cleric', for he had acquired a position as a 'cleric', i.e. a theologian. His ancestor — also named Klingsor — had once been sent to the king of Hungary from his centre of activity in Terra de Labur.

We come up against a mysterious stream which extends over centuries. It starts with the magician whose castle at Chastelmerveil had been built to be a centre of opposition to the Grail Castle, and leads us to the young Klingsor whose influence was felt in minstrel circles. The poem about the Minstrels' Contest actually mirrors the spiritual struggle at the turn of the epoch. Around the year 1200, Wolfram, the representative of the Christian West, fights with the 'sword of the Grail' against the Arabic inheritance of cosmic mysteries. At the turn of the thirteenth century, there was as yet no accord between Christianity and the wisdom of the East. The union between Parzival and Feirefiz at the end of Wolfram's poem can be seen as a presage of future development. For under no circumstances should Christianity renounce the quest for cosmic wisdom. But it was for Rudolf Steiner to rediscover the cosmic dimension of Christianity, which had been lost in Wolfram's time.

We can further illuminate the Klingsor image by a geographical-geological consideration of Sicily, and in particular, the rocky castle of Caltabellotta. This stood at the beginning of Friedrich Häusler's articles, which were the prelude of his 1937 book *Das Rätsel Sizilien* ('The Sicilian Riddle').[10] The island is the geographical centre of Mediterranean culture, and Caltabellotta has a special geological position. Sulphur and salt are found there on top of each other — the very materials which are the symbols of opposing forces for the alchemist.

From history, we know the intimate connection between Sicily and the Hohenstaufen family, in particular the connection of Henry VI with Caltabellotta. In the struggle against the Norman king whose duke Tancred had died, Caltabellotta fell into the hands of the Emperor. Tancred's widow Sybil and her children had gone there for protection, following the advice of her brother Richard of Acerra. Sybil was banished to Odilienberg in Alsace; the under-age son was castrated and blinded. Ernst Uehli speaks

of the 'powerful, all-dominating chiaroscuro of the Hohenstaufen', who were familiar both with the Grail and with the anti-
Grail.[11]

Günther Wachsmuth's legacy, the drama he composed about
Emperor Frederic II entitled *Erzengel im Konzil* ('The Archangel in
the Council'), describes the Caltabellotta milieu. The first scene
starts with a conversation between Sybil and a Benedictine monk
from Chartres:

> *Monk*: Do I hear human cries, my Queen?
>
> *Sybil (indifferently)*: They are being tortured in the cellar. Fear
> and suffering are magic substances which we use.
>
> *Monk*: Where am I?
>
> *Sybil*: In Klingsor's kingdom. The castle of Caltabellotta on the
> rock, from which you can see Africa and Asia. It is unfamiliar to
> you in the north... In Klingsor's kingdom, victory does not come
> through courage. We force our opponents on to their knees with
> fear. People here believe in Mohammed, learn wisdom from
> Gondishapur, from Arabia. We serve Lucifer and the goddess
> Iblis.

Of course, neither the name of Klingsor nor that of Iblis are
to be found in the medieval chronicles. But every crusader
knew it: Iblis is the daughter of Eblis, and Eblis is the Muslim
name of the leader of the fallen angels, Lucifer. Iblis, therefore,
is the feminine aspect of the luciferic. The contemporaries who
understood Wolfram's poetry might well ask: Why did Klingsor ally himself with the fallen spirits? And who is the secret
bearer of Klingsor's name? In those days, one understood history from top to bottom, i.e. they knew what we now must
learn all over again, that historical events are the imprecise
casts of primitive spiritual images, more or less successful performances of divine symphonies. Whoever had an awareness
about history at that time knew which role was assigned to
them in the mystery drama of history. Whoever understood
Wolfram knew: light-filled streams of life flow out of the Grail,
which have vouchsafed spiritual progress ever since Golgotha.
The counter-forces spread the anti-Gospel from the seat of

Iblis, from Klingsor's castle. And whoever begins to understand Rudolf Steiner will know the difference between the Christian impulse and the spiritual forces that are opposed to it.

We can now take the last step, and ask for Rudolf Steiner's interpretation of the Klingsor forces. We will use here the karma lecture of 18 September 1924 (CW 354) and the last lecture in the cycle *Mysteries of the East and of Christianity* (February 1913, CW 144).

The karma lecture contains the quintessence of what Rudolf Steiner had to say: the Master Cleric from Hungary is the knower of the old astral wisdom. He is the representative of a 'dechristianized cosmology of the Middle Ages', which contrasts with Wolfram's 'star-less' Christianity. He is also the 'blackest' magician of his time.

But the decisive element, the key for our subject, is in the cycle *Mysteries of the East and of Christianity*. There Steiner speaks of the enemies of the Grail and the extent of their power. The influence of this opposition to the Grail extends from Terra de Labur in southern Italy through the straits into Sicily, and from there makes its way into the rest of Europe. Whatever evil comes out of this centre is articulated around the legendary figure of Klingsor, legendary but 'quite familiar to anyone interested in the mysteries'. His 'evil influences' can be felt even now in Sicily. The tie between Klingsor and Iblis is 'of all the dangerous ties which were established in the course of the Earth's development between beings with occult powers ... the most dangerous'.

Historically speaking, the Klingsor stream appears as a spiritual superpower of oriental origin that works with magic tools. It arises in an unchristian form (a form not appropriate for the times), spreading the spirit of un-freedom and working far into the future.

The following questions now arise. Where do the Klingsor powers take root in the human being? How do they attack? And where do they penetrate? The answers can be found if the situation of modern man can be clarified through an intimate science of man and radical self-knowledge. Rudolf Steiner adds to this: occult vision allows one to recognize 'dead enclosures' in the physical and etheric body, 'dead organs in the physical body', 'parts that have become unconscious in the realm of the soul', so to speak. This reality can be traced to the constitution of human consciousness in the Egypto-Chaldean culture. 'All of today's souls once looked out into the universe and received spiritual impressions the way we now receive the impressions of colour and tone. It is there at the ground of the soul, and, from it, souls build bodies for themselves. But souls have forgotten it.'

We are thus talking about 'forgotten spiritual impressions, about unconscious imaginations which were received in an Egypto-Chaldean incarnation'. The deeper layers of the soul lay closer to the surface in those days. They have lost meaning for our modern objective consciousness. These layers of the soul, where depth-psychology looks for archetypes, can work positively as well as negatively, depending on their 'allegiance'. They are targeted by the Klingsor forces, which send their luciferic and ahrimanic forces into the field. While the luciferic element works 'more spiritually', forging pseudo-ideals, the ahrimanic works more from the subconscious, in so far as it floods the consciousness and seizes the will. The forces of the Grail work in precisely the opposite way. They teach people to dominate the 'deadened parts of the physical body' and to reconquer what has become unconscious in the etheric body.

Through the cultic-ritualistic methods we have described, National Socialism brought back to life the 'enclosure'. The older layers of the soul were galvanized and, in so doing, destructive forces were released. Thus started the psychic epidemic of mass hysteria, whose markers are failures to recognize reality and relative incorrigibility. One could observe it work like the spread of a plague. Whoever was attacked lost the eye for reality, and closed himself to his better insights. Klingsor forces scourged the German people with this plague.

The fraud was enormous. At first the destructive impulse appeared under the guise of construction. Autobahns, elimination of unemployment, 'strength through joy', national community—these were Klingsor's wondrous gardens, designed to mislead the seekers for the Grail. But the phantom came to an abrupt end, and the quote from Wagner's *Parsifal* was realized: 'The lying splendour collapses in grief and ruins.' In retrospect, one can see the interaction of the two tempters: Lucifer took the role of seducer; Ahriman finished the job. But let us not delude ourselves! The Klingsor forces have been defeated but not annihilated. It is hoped that we will recognize them in their new disguise, for their strongest weapons are camouflage, fraud, stupor. Rudolf Steiner speaks of the most dangerous forces of oriental magic. We have seen them as the decadent astrological-magical praxis of the East, which made its way into Germany through the channels Sebottendorf, Haushofer and Gurdjieff.

But the Klingsor aspect and the Sorat aspect do not quite suffice to throw light on the spiritual battlefield. There is one more theme we will speak about in conclusion. It is also accessible to the broadening field of experience of modern man, who has been led by destiny into borderline situations or who has, by his own efforts, reached the threshold of experience. Whoever walks into the perimeter of the spiritual world comes straight away into the vicinity of the dragon, 'the old snake, which is there called Diabolos and Satan'. But the effective power of the evil that wants to upset and destroy is met by a strengthening of the forces of good, which want to save and heal.

We start from soul-observations that can be made following the thread of anthroposophical cognition. As a result of his diagnosis of the modern cultural crisis, Rudolf Steiner came to the conclusion that mankind as a whole will pass unconsciously over the threshold of the spiritual world. What does that mean? The myths of antiquity contain initiate-knowledge about the conditions for crossing into Hades, which leads people over the threshold. They transmit this knowledge in the language of picturesque and dramatic events which must be seen as illustrative of spiritual experiences, as the precipitate of soul experiences. For instance, the *Odyssey* shows the stages of a man who searches for a way back into the 'homeland' and who eventually succeeds in his goal, having held his ground in the trials of anxiety about living, homelessness and extreme distress over destiny, and in the encounter with death and with evil. It is the description of a path of initiation.

Such experiences today come up as consciousness-experiences. However, they usually have neither the intensity nor the lawful order in which they were presented to the spiritual candidate. Think of the experiences destined for the twentieth century: the rampant fear of a Third World War, the fear of nuclear weapons and of Bolshevism; the sense of homelessness which has overcome many; the anxiety about destiny, in earlier times a privilege of the upper classes but now at the disposal of anybody; the death of millions since 1933; the coldness and the proximity to death in an over-technological civilization; the encounter with the double nature of evil; and finally, the schizophrenic manifestations which progress at an alarming rate.[12]

Not only do we live in the time of the splitting of the atom; it was preceded by the fission of the soul, which had been heralded for a long time. Rudolf Steiner had shown its presence in Goethe, who produced poetry of the first rank while displaying highly questionable frailties. 'In older times, the two natures were never split so far apart.'[13] The splitting of the personality has turned into an epidemic. The natural interconnection of thinking, feeling and will has been loosened. And when it ruptures there appears the threefold aberration: the man of violence; the glutton for feeling; the cold seeker of wisdom. This is the scenery of the threshold, which can be seen on the stage of history.

In this hour of great crisis, where humanity's fate is being decided, the new call of the Baptist, the new call of John, goes out to our contemporaries, and it is a condensation of anthroposophy: 'Change your souls! For the egos of human beings have matured enough to rise into the higher worlds.'

What can those matured egos experience? In the realm of soul experience new possibilities of tremendous importance have arisen. Man can rise consciously from thinking to seeing. The new contemplative seeing is acquired by individual efforts along the path of anthroposophical schooling, which proceeds from Imagination through Inspiration to Intuition. In due course, contemplative vision can appear as a natural force, a supposedly natural or etheric clairvoyance whose role is to make itself into an organ for the perception of the etheric Christ. The first public reference to this capacity was the Rosicrucian mystery play *The Portal of Initiation* (GA 14), when the experiences of the seer Theodora are described.

These possibilities, which can push through and come to completion, are the legitimate paths into the spiritual world, appropriate for our time. Aside from them, there are older, no longer adequate practices. We have come to know two of these decadent forms: the 'mediumistic' experience in conditions of trance or half-trance; and, the oriental methods which Sebottendorf, Haushofer and Gurdjieff learnt and mastered.

The new paths to spiritual knowledge have an inner connection with the appearance of Christ in the etheric. This cannot be stopped. That is why the enemies of whom we speak attempt to block the new possibilities. Klingsor's and Sorat's attacks are an attempt to darken the Parousia for mankind, the 'light' of the 'age of light'. The adversary's enormous display of power started in the second third of the twentieth century. It arrived precisely at the point in time when the new capacities of etheric clairvoyance revealed themselves.

Rudolf Steiner first mentioned this in 1910. On 25 January he lectured in Karlsruhe: 'The first signs of these new soul faculties will soon begin to appear in isolated individuals. Those signs will become clearer during the fourth decade, between 1930 and 1940, and especially in 1933, 1935 and 1937. Faculties that are still rare in people will begin to manifest as natural abilities. Along with this, there will be great changes; biblical prophecies will be fulfilled. Everything will be transformed for those on earth as well as for those who are no longer in a physical body. Regardless of where they are, souls are meeting entirely new faculties. Everything is changing...'

The biblical prophecies have to do with the bodily appearance of the Antichrist and the spiritual return of Christ. The most important statement is in St Paul's Epistle to the Thessalonians: 'For He will not come, unless the man of sins be revealed, the child of destruction.'

The dark forces can only succeed in so far as the light of the light-filled age is on the rise.[14] At first, the dark forces ruled the historical stage. Mass psychosis of the soul broke out, the 'abomination of desolation' started (Matthew 24:15); demons were prayed to. But we have no justice. What happened is so monstrous as to remain beyond human responsibility or jurisdiction. Our duty, as far as we are able, is to overcome evil by building monuments of cognition.

> The master of destiny does not want
> For you to raise your hand in judgement
> Only that you live in truth
> The spirit itself is the judgement.

These lines by Albert Steffen are the development of a line in St John's Apocalypse: 'Behold, I will come soon. The reward which I give, I will be myself: to each a destiny which corresponds to his actions.'

In his lecture 'Christ in the Etheric World', Herbert Hahn spoke about a 'hidden chronicle of the new Christ experiences'.[15] Many are plunged in this hidden stream, but few have reported on them. In his mystery poem 'Gold and Midnight', Alexander von Bernus writes the following:

> In order to partake of the Son of the Sun
> For the sake of this instant we will live
> All our lives.

The doctor and curative psychologist Karl König, during the course of Advent 1965, gave a lecture titled, 'The History and Destiny of the Jewish People'.[16] His descriptions touch upon the deep karmic consequences which came out of the historical concatenation between the Germans and the Jews. The contours of this world-historic problem are barely discernible. But it is possible to interpret the language of events, and König has started to decipher the historical hieroglyphs in relation to these two peoples: Israel in the first millennium BC, between the two empires of Egypt and Babylon; and Germany nowadays, between the world powers of America and Russia. After 50 years of Babylonian exile, the tribes of Judah and Benjamin were allowed to return to the Holy Land, after having followed the call of the prophets and encountered in the depths of their humiliation the great teacher, the younger Zarathustra. Will the Germans hear the voice of their prophets, the representatives of Goethe's time? Will they meet the great Rudolf Steiner? Is Goethe right in saying, 'The Germans will have to be uprooted and dispersed like the Jews throughout the world, in order to develop the measure of good and healing which lies in them'? Today, Germany is a geographical concept, a collection of towns, states, provinces, under two governments,* without any real direction. Germany's destiny can no longer have a geopolitical solution, but only a spiritual one. Since 1945, the historical landscape we live in has been completely altered. Power politics are over. Educating the historical conscience will be necessary. Its voice will stir with the new call of John the Baptist: 'Change your souls! For the egos of mankind are mature enough to rise into the higher worlds.'

---

* East and West Germany. This book was written during the Cold War division of Europe.

Appendix: The *Völkische Beobachter* and Rudolf Steiner

Documentations which throw light on the opposition between the Nazi movement and anthroposophy after World War I, compiled and annotated by Andreas Bracher

I. Preliminary Remarks

A number of articles or extracts from articles in issues of the *Völkische Beobachter* of 1921 and 1922, which are concerned in one way or another with Rudolf Steiner, are quoted in the following.[1] The intention is to show — in the contemporary context of allegations against Steiner and the anthroposophical movement* — what the true nature of the relationship between anthroposophy and nascent National Socialism entailed. The *Völkische Beobachter* ('People's Observer'), originating from the *Münchener Beobachter* which had been bought up in 1918 by Sebottendorf, founder of the Thule Society, was the journal of the 'Anti-Semites', i.e. the emerging *völkisch* movement which from 1921 onwards found its centre in the NSDAP (National Socialist German Workers Party). From 1933 until 1945 this was the most important newspaper in Hitler's Germany, the Third Reich, acting as the mouthpiece of both Party and Government. Viewed from today, it is remarkable to note how thoroughly the spirit that ruled Germany after 1933 was already present in the *Völkische Beobachter* at the beginning of the 1920s. Even then, Nazism had already 'arrived', and all it had to do was win over society as a whole together with the state as such. All the articles are already steeped in anti-Semitic polemics. Jewry as the opponent and hate-object was the connecting link that bound the diverging streams of the *völkisch* movement together. The anti-Semitic litany was its mantra.

The articles exhibit several external traces of the campaign

---

* See, for example, Peter Staudenmaier, *Between Occultism and Nazism*, Brill 2013.

which was set in motion against anthroposophy by the *völkisch* movement after World War I. The controversy that took place between the anti-Semitic *völkisch* movement and the anthroposophical movement between 1919 and 1922 could be described as the 'battle for the soul of Germany'. Its significance reaches way beyond the relative marginality of the two movements at the time. The immediate concerns were ideas for Germany's political and social future: on the one hand a total exaggeration of the centralized state as called for by the *völkisch* movement, and on the other the threefold division of the state into the spheres of rights, economy and culture as independent members, as proposed by Rudolf Steiner. The weekly journal *Dreigliederung des sozialen Organismus*, which between 1919 and 1922 was the most important published organ of the anthroposophical movement in Germany, demonstrates very clearly that the main front opposing and mocking social threefolding came from right-wing factions. From the side of the *völkisch* movement the battle consisted chiefly of libelous and inaccurate remarks, calling Rudolf Steiner 'anti-German', or suggesting he was Jewish or Hungarian,[*] and so on. The articles in the *Völkische Beobachter* clearly demonstrate the hatred with which Steiner was viewed from that quarter.

One aspect of the conflict consisted in opposite views about Germany's and the German people's role in the world. Steiner considered that it was their mission to be citizens of the world, as understood in the context of threefolding, while the view of the *völkisch* movement was that Germany was superior and should cut its psychological ties with foreign countries. Was Germany supposed to have a specific role of service to mankind or of domination over it? It is not surprising, but tragic, that it was the more flattering but less challenging mood of the *völkisch* movement—Germans as the *Herrenvolk*—which prevailed at that time. At the end of 1922, with a sure sense for what was happening, the *Völkische Beobachter* declared Rudolf Steiner 'dead' for Germany. Threefolding as a potential mass movement had failed and the

---

[*] The Nazis, of course, considered Jews, Slavs and most East Europeans to be sub-human.

climate in Germany made it impossible for him to continue lecturing there. It is remarkable to note the accuracy with which *völkisch* circles took note of this situation and the degree of satisfaction evidenced as a result. (See Extract 6.)

II. Additional explanations regarding the content of the articles

Steiner had considered it of paramount importance to prevent inclusion in the Treaty of Versailles – the peace treaty drawn up at the end of World War I – of the passage about the sole culpability of Germany and her allies, the so-called 'War Guilt Clause' (article 231). And that clause did indeed became the basis for all the demands made on Germany for reparations, and also a chief point of attack in the behaviour of Germany's right wing after 1919. In order to counteract that codification, Steiner spoke up for complete openness on the part of Germany about all that had been happening when war broke out.[2] He expected this to show that there had clearly been no cold-blooded, long-term desire for conflict leading to Germany's declaration of war on 1 August 1914.

In this connection Steiner had, in May 1919, been preparing for the publication of a short article in which the German Chief of General Staff, Helmuth von Moltke, described the processes at work in Berlin when war broke out in 1914. Publication of that article, accompanied by a foreword by Steiner, was thwarted at the last moment by the German Supreme Army Command who had been notified about its imminent publication and who claimed that it contained factual errors.[*]

However, the actual background appears to have been that this publication may very well have led to a different understanding outside Germany of Germany's declaration of war, but that within Germany it could have destabilized the position of

---

[*] See further in T.H. Meyer (Ed.), *Light for the New Millennium*, Rudolf Steiner Press 1997.

the whole (old) military and political élite because it would have brought to light all the instability and bumbling incompetence of their actions. The Supreme Army Command evidently preferred to maintain their position within Germany rather than improve Germany's standing internationally.

It appears to have been this process – after a series of metamorphoses – that finally led to Steiner being accused of wanting to betray German officers to the Entente, as shown here later in several articles. In reality Steiner had no intention of 'betraying' German officers to other countries; but he had taken steps which made certain officers nervous that their incompetence could be 'betrayed' to the German population. (See articles 4, 5 and 6.)

The polemical style of the *Völkische Beobachter* was definitively shaped by Dietrich Eckart (1868–1923) who was chief editor from mid-1921 to early 1923. His successor was Alfred Rosenberg, subsequently the Nazis' chief ideologue, who had been trained by Eckart as a journalist. From 1918 to 1920 Eckart had published the journal *Auf gut Deutsch* ('In proper German fashion'), honing his anti-Semitic style the while. He had also published two detailed articles in which Steiner even then was already made the target of attacks.[3]

The *Völkische Beobachter* became, under Eckart, the propaganda journal of the NSDAP, which in turn had become the central organization of the *völkisch* movement. It was also Eckart who began to refer to Hitler as 'der Führer' in the *Beobachter*. Eckart was a Catholic, which was typical of a large proportion of those joining the *völkisch* movement. Without the (psychological) basis of that Catholicism, it would be impossible to comprehend the movement and why so many of its protagonists stemmed from Austria, and also why Munich, of all places, became its centre in Germany.

The *Völkische Beobachter* followed the well-tried system of running campaigns aimed at specific politicians who were each symbolically singled out and bombarded with hatred in a series of articles. Objects of this hatred in 1921 and 1922 were the Reich Foreign Minister Simons (1861–1937) who was targeted as one of those who believed that the stipulations of Versailles should be upheld, the Bavarian Minister-President Count Lerchenfeld because he opposed the *völkisch* movement too strongly in Bavaria, and Walther Rathenau (1867–1922) who, as Simons' successor and as an industrialist, a politician and a Jew, was quintessentially suited to be targeted. It is interesting to note that both Simons and Lerchenfeld, two of those three hate symbols of the *Beobachter*, were also brought into a connection with Steiner. Simons was described as a pupil of Steiner, and in the case of Lerchenfeld it was noted that one of his brothers was a close collaborator of Steiner. This may support the thesis that the *völkisch* movement at that time was clearly homing in on Steiner as a principal enemy whose influence in Germany would have to be curtailed if their own influence were to prevail. (See articles 1 and 3.)

Threefolding was considered or at least portrayed by the *völkisch* movement to be a variation of 'communism' or 'Bolshevism'. Decisive in the rejection of threefolding was, among much else, that it represented the principle of 'equality' or the 'equal rights' of all individuals, i.e. equality before the law. *Völkisch* anti-Semites, on the other hand, were aiming to include racial criteria in the law, which became reality with the passing of the Nuremberg Race Laws in 1935.

III. *Articles and extracts*

Article 1: 15.3.1921: *Staatsmänner oder Novemberverbrecher* ('Statesmen or November criminals'), by A. Hitler.

Preliminary note: The following article was written against the background of the London Conference (21.2-14.3.1921), one of the conferences which discussed the amounts of and procedures for regulating the reparation payments Germany was expected to make in accordance with the Versailles Treaty.

Extract: 'In London a man sent by the German people to represent them, to their own misfortune, declares himself prepared to accept a treaty which signifies the full enslavement and thus annihilation of Germany. In any half-decent state such an enterprise would have earned that man a summons to attend the State Constitutional Court. Indeed, in countries with more primitive and thus healthier sensibilities the reply would have arrived in the form of a silken thread. In Germany one pretends to the people that the Minister has fulfilled his duty to the nation in full measure and voices the gratitude of the nation to that unprincipled dealer. [...]

'It can only be described as utter brazenness when this Herr Simons, who is not a pre-March liberal but an employee of the German people, takes it upon himself to declare that the German people are incapable of assessing their own potential to pay. Perhaps Simons is indeed more capable of doing this, for he has estimated the German people's potential to pay as being very considerable. As the business in London proceeds, some very mysterious attendant circumstances are gradually appearing, so that it is becoming necessary to have a closer look at this Minister, intimate friend of the Gnostic and Anthroposophist Rudolf Steiner, supporter of a threefolding of the social organism and whatever else all those Jewish methods call themselves that want to destroy the normal state of mind among the nations. Perhaps a mindless look is, as Loyd George [sic] would have it, indeed merely the result of mindlessness, or could it be that it is a disguise behind which other things are hidden?'

Article 2: 31.7.1921: *Kampf!* ('Battle!') by Alfred Rosenberg.

Preliminary note: Karl Heise was a strangely unfortunate figure on the outer fringes of the anthroposophical movement who at the same time also sought contact with the völkisch *movement. This desire for contact was based partly on affinities within Heise's thinking (which was not representative of the anthroposophical movement), and also partly on misjudgements or illusions. It was his endeavours to demonstrate 'true occultism', i.e. anthroposophy, to the* völkisch *movement that caused him to be sent packing.*[4]

Extract: 'The editor's office recently received an enquiry from Herr Karl Heise (author of *Ententefreimaurerei und der Weltkrieg,*

"Freemasonry of Entente and the world war") asking whether they would consider publishing an occultistic essay penned by him. Only "true occultism" could save Germany, he maintained. Herr Heise's offer was declined.

'Artur Tinter used to be an outstanding fighter against Jewry. *Used to be*, for now he writes books about table rapping and preaches a "spiritual doctrine" remarkably reminiscent of the present Grand Cophta*, Rudolf Steiner. We are waiting for him to turn away from this once more and regain his health.

'It is up to us to reject all such nebulousness. We recognize solely the national character of the German people as a foundation and a starting point; we recognize only Germanness and Greater Germany as our ultimate goal. We recognize only ideas and ideals that boost our strength and steel our will so that we may tread the path upon which we have met one another without having to take note of a pack of enemies and friends who have become feeble.'

Article 3: 19.10.1921: *Programmgemäss* ('According to the programme')

Preliminary note: The following extract is written against the background of the change of Bavarian Minister-President from Gustav von Kahr to Count Hugo von Lerchenfeld-Köfering (Bavarian Minister-President from 21.9.1921 to 2.11.1922). Von Kahr had been popular with the far right. He had caused Bavaria to become a centre of reactionary nationalism, 'Bavaria – Cell of Order'. Although also politically at home on the right (BVP), von Lerchenfeld was not attracted to the völkisch *movement. Hugo von Lerchenfeld (*1871) was the younger brother of Otto Count Lerchenfeld (*1868) whose question asked in 1917 had led to Steiner's outline of threefolding. Both were nephews of the Hugo von Lerchenfeld (1843–1925), who had been Bavarian Ambassador to the Reich in Berlin from 1880 to 1919.*

Extract: 'Everyone has noticed it; whomever you ask amongst ordinary folk, they all say the same: "Of course it's the Jew! He

---

* A reference to Goethe's comedy *Der Groß-Cophta* (1791).

caused the war and the revolution. He robbed us blind, and now he's got us by the throat!''

'All those who are still in possession of their five senses know it. Only the ones who ought to know it first and foremost, Dr Wirth, Stegewalt, Count Lerchenfeld, Dr Heim, the Schweners, the Heids, and Hamms and so on, it seems, haven't got the faintest idea; and yet they go on playing at being the leaders, talking the hind leg off a donkey, putting their heads together, whispering for all they're worth whilst carrying us along inexorably on their so-called "middle way" to our final fate: Bolshevist chaos. [...]

'From the *Red Flag* and on to the *Frankfurter Zeitung* and the *Munich News*, there resounded, either openly or somewhat more hidden, a cry of joy when underground machinations without compare succeeded in replacing Herr von Kahr with that shady character Count Lerchenfeld. In other words, all the Jewish rags in the world couldn't contain themselves in their delight about the changeover. And yet the *Bavarian Courier*, that organ of the centre, has the audacity to claim that everything is the same as before and there has been no change of direction?! What the devil do these people take us for? For baboons, or merino sheep? Or do they in the end think that the Jews have all of a sudden lost their infallible instinct and can no longer tell an *ox* from an *ass*?

'Thus far, *Graf Lerchenfeld* has not spoken a single word against that great evil, *Judaism*; and neither will he as long as he lives, you can be sure! That alone is the crux of the matter. And therein lies the fly in the ointment: the very brother of the one who has for years been supporting Rudolf Steiner, "that gallant communist", as though he were the Messiah, is not for nothing Israel's favourite.'

Article 4. 27.5.1922: *Steiner, der neue Messias* (Steiner, the New Messiah), by W-a.

Preliminary note: The following exhaustive article was Part 3 of a block in the Völkische Beobachter *about so-called polluters of the German people. Under this heading the journal also dealt with 'serious Bible scholars' (Jehovah's Witnesses), 'Theosophists', and modern art (Picasso). On 15.5.1922, i.e. 12 days before publication of this article, a lecture had been given by Steiner in Munich during which it had been necessary for a protection force to shield him against a group of völkisch thugs. The article refers briefly to that lecture. It also refers to various points about which Eckart had written elsewhere in 1919. The author does not know the identity of 'W-a'.*

Extract: 'If even Theosophy, the mother, is of doubtful descent and tainted repute, what can be said of her son, the anthroposophist *Dr Steiner*? The apple does not fall far from the tree. We know Steiner's mother. But as for the father, that is a different matter. He is said not to have been a Jew, but anyone examining the crippled forms of Steiner's thinking will not find it hard to discern in them that Talmud and Kabbala were the sperms from which this peculiar growth emerged. So what is it that Steiner wants? Well, more or less what the Theosophists want. It is simply a touch more ambitious and somewhat more generous with its promises, it sparkles more, and he is more adept at beating his own drum for his thoughts than are his theosophical brothers. On the whole, *Dr Franz Hartmann* has summarized what Steiner talks of very well: "What is good in what Steiner brings is not new, and what is new in what Steiner brings is not good." In other words and less tactfully expressed: Steiner's joyful message is stolen from all over, is partially understood and knocked together before being thrown before the masses as though straight from the factory. This factory element is its essential characteristic, since Herr Steiner, as a modern saint, is also a very talented businessman. He has linked his *Spiritual Science* with a *Joint Stock Company* "Der Kommende Tag" ("The coming day"). And even though twilight has suddenly broken in on that coming day on account of *unholy* happenings, the company's capital of 70 million proved that Spiritual Science is in credit. But now to the teachings of this apostle. By means of *contemplative exercises*, Herr Steiner has attained *clairvoyance*. In this way he has reached "knowledge of higher worlds" which he now wants to make available here in Germany, after the pattern of his "threefold ordering of the social organism", through the cigarette factory Waldorf-Astoria and other "earthly worlds" bound together in *Der Kommende Tag*. In this higher world which "Der Kommende Tag" will bring to us, the rule of course is *equal rights for all*, so "through the rising up of the lower orders, specifically those known as the proletariat, we may now expect a new cultural flowering". So Herr Steiner, like his theosophical brethren, is a noble Bolshevist; he is flirting with their international state and has already thought out how he can render its enemies harmless.

'He is "advising urgently that the following be organized: that the names of all officers be obtained who are or might be in any way working in a reactionary way". After this, false witnesses would have to be found who "would have to go on record under oath according to which the officers would be said to have committed acts in contravention of international law against the population of the enemy [...] This conclusion would have to be passed on to the *Freemasonry of the Entente*." We owe this information to *Der Hammer* No. 466, and it has to date not been contradicted. So we see that Herr Steiner is also a politician after the manner of someone like Eisner whom he also resembles, in that through his paper *To the German people and the civilized world* he casts the moral blame for the world war on to Germany.

'One's pencil bristles at having to concern itself in earnest with such a Germany-hating charlatan. But one's hair bristles even more when one considers that this person was able to give a lecture in Munich last week without any intervention by the government! Or was it perhaps not possible for the Bavarian government to interfere with the work of this enemy of the people because of its close ties with him on account of the fact that Herr Otto von Lerchenfeld is a co-founder of the spiritual-scientific joint stock company "Der Kommende Tag"? This would not surprise us because a large number of worshippers and patrons of Steiner are also busy making mischief in the *Foreign Office* in Berlin.

'To sum up: In fact what Herr Steiner wants to achieve through his teachings is no different from what all the enemies of our state and our German people also want. He merely has another name for it. He pursues his murky business under the name of "Anthroposophy" and "Threefolding", and he has millions at his disposal with which to pollute our German people through his teachings. Through his influence over the widest circles he has become a threat to both our present and our future. Let him spray his poison in other countries if he so wishes, for example in Dornach near Basel, where he has built a temple for himself with the name of which he has defiled our Goethe, that very Goethe who wrote to Lavater in 1781: "Believe me, our moral and political world is undermined by subterranean passages, cellars and sewers." Sewer is a word that suits Herr Steiner's environment very well where, as a reincarnated Christ, he expected his 21 reincarnated Magdalenes to lick his hands.'

Article 5. 17.6.1922: *Der 'berichtigte' Steiner* (Steiner 'amended')

Extract: 'With reference to our article "Steiner, the New Messiah" in No. 42 of our journal, the "Threefold Social Order Association" has sent us a correction stating that it is untrue that the revelations published in *Der Hammer* had not been contradicted. The "threefolders" also say that anyway Rudolf Steiner's name does not appear in the secret text which *Der Hammer* has published. The logic of this anthroposophical correction is, however, shown up by its final sentence: "The fact that certain journals do not, or only incompletely, print corrections sent to them does not prove that the imputations have not been contradicted."

'The decision made by *Der Hammer* not to publish the corrections received from the threefolders, *which we fully stand by*, was based on the following (see *Der Hammer* No. 468): 1. The "Threefold Social Order Association" is not authorized to represent Dr Steiner; 2. Since there is a contradiction between what the "official" source presents and what the Threefold Association claims, absolute credence must be given to the official source; only *legal proceedings* can annul or render this invalid.

'We were not concerned with the "Threefold Social Order Association", behind which Herr Steiner is hiding; we are saving for another issue our discussion of the nonsense they proclaim. If he feels that he is implicated, that is his affair. What we are concerned with is Herr Steiner. For us his silence and his shadow pantomime behind the scenes of "threefolding" is more in need of being watched than are corrections from the scene shifters. We are of course not surprised by this behaviour since it has always been the wont of this new Messiah to ward off any valid criticism and instead let his disciples and apostles take the blame.'

Article 6: 21.10.1922: *Die vergangene Nacht von Kraljewitz* ('The bygone night of Kraljevec')

Extract: 'Once upon a time there was a "coming day" [reference to *Der Kommende Tag*], but the sun that should have shone on ahead of it proved to be a nightlight, and under the cover of darkness the night-watchmen altered the company's name and called it "Association for Free Spiritual Life". The man whose life free of spirit was meant, Herr Rudolf Steiner, now finally scientifically done for, cannot overcome his regret that no-one is seriously interested in him any longer; so, keeping himself in the background as usual, he makes sure his faithful worshippers are once again attracting attention.

'The battle is entirely transparent. It is directed not against the cause and the arguments of the opponents but against their person and in the crassness of its method does not even shrink from including the opponents' family circumstances as well. In No.3 of the journal *Anthroposophy* — formerly known as *The Threefold Social Order* — Retired Captain *von Grone* devotes all of eight pages to Steiner's most dangerous opponent, General *Gerold von Gleich*. It is not necessary to go into detail, especially since von Grone's style of doing battle makes it impossible for any decent human being to enter into conflict on the same patch. Herr Grone of course returns to the accusation previously stated in *Der Hammer* regarding Steiner's betrayal of German officers' names to the Entente, without adding anything substantially new since of course the final verdict would have to be given by a court of law to which Steiner would have to apply for a resolution of the question.

'To date this has not been done, and von Grone's claim that the letters published in *Der Hammer* are forgeries therefore lacks any proof. The Steinerites are of course aware of this and so they have put forward von Grone and Count Bothmer to settle the matter by means of an *affaire d'honneur* with General Gerold von Gleich. This, too, is indicative of the "genteel" modus operandi of the "Association for Free Spiritual Life". After all, it has hitherto always been customary for an *affaire d'honneur* between officers not to be conducted in public through the pages of a newspaper.

'The prophet from Kraljevec is dead for Germany. He is no doubt aware of this, for at present he is practising his quackery on the English upon whom we are only too glad to wish a dozen such jesters. It is furthermore pleasing to note that his adherents in Germany are also beginning to dig their graves — at least a sign that the soul of our German people is beginning to recover. We can congratulate retired captain von Grone on being the first to die for Steiner. In the next issue of *Anthroposophy* there will no doubt be further disciples of the Master who will make themselves appear *outrageous*.'

IV. Postscript

We may look upon threefolding as a culmination of the cultural epoch of Goethe's era, creating a broadening of social thinking to which Goetheanism itself could not yet have aspired. It gave a modern, in its time contemporary, expression to the supranational facet of the Germans, the people of the old Reich, which was otherwise not yet in keeping with a unitary, centralized state.

Although threefolding as such can be understood as the fundamental social truth of the fifth post-Atlantean age, the epoch of the consciousness soul, Rudolf Steiner put it forward after World War I as being specifically suitable for Central Europe and Germany. With the World War lost, he considered the situation in Central Europe to be especially uncertain: 'For Central Europe the situation was a matter of life and death, the life and death of the national character. [...] It is now, absolutely for the very immediate future, a matter of either-or: there is either a comprehension of threefolding or the death of the national German character.'[5] In speaking of the 'death of the national German character', Steiner did not mean physical annihilation.

From this point of view one can sense the very profound degree of resignation that must have led to the need to declare in 1922 that the threefold movement had failed and was to be abandoned. It therefore appears doubly significant that the main resistance to threefolding came from the *völkisch*-National Socialist movement, even though its failure has to be explained chiefly on the basis of internal inadequacies. The national German character which Steiner described in 1919 as being endangered was then indeed destroyed during the twelve years of the Third Reich. Those mass rallies, the party congresses, marches, gatherings and torch-lit processions etc., with their grimly earnest pomp, so profoundly enjoyed at such a deep level, were in fact its funeral rites, celebrating with rapture and brutal doggedness its own suicide.

Bibliography

Recent works on the occult aspects of National Socialism,
compiled and annotated by Andreas Bracher

Johannes Tautz's book remains as yet the most successful approach both to reaching an understanding of National Socialism as a genuine spiritual phenomenon and to analysing its origins and its symptomatology. Nevertheless, as did Tautz himself, we must still consider this work to be an initial endeavour at comprehension. This is so not only in the matter of comprehending the phenomenon historically but also of gaining a more profound understanding of it *per se*.

Below is a compilation of works which have appeared in recent decades on the themes also discussed by Tautz. This compilation does not claim to be complete. The brief characterizations are intended to highlight the very varying interests and backgrounds of the authors.

Wilfried Daim, *Der Mann, der Hitler die Ideen gab — Jörg Lanz von Lie-benfels* ('The man who gave Hitler his ideas — Jörg Lanz von Lie-benfels'), 3rd Edition, Vienna 1994 (330pp).

Seminal biography of Lanz by a Viennese psychoanalyst who also endeavours to give a psychoanalytical interpretation of Lanz's and Hitler's patterns of thought. This book is sometimes rather eccentric. It is also hampered by the limitations posed by the psychoanalytic view and tends to over-estimate Lanz's role.

Friedrich W. Doucet, *Im Banne des Mythos — die Psychologie des Dritten Reiches* ('Mesmerized by the myth — the psychology of the Third Reich'), Esslingen 1979 (296 pp)

An interpretation of the Third Reich in which motivations and symbolism are investigated on the basis of depth and social psychology. Its tendency is to warn against underestimating the depths which the Third Reich stirred up in people through its symbolism. The author sometimes treads the narrow path of himself becoming fascinated by that symbolism.

Joscelyn Godwin, *Arktos: Polar Myth in Science, Symbolism and Nazi Survival*, Adventures Unlimited Press, 1996

A historical and philological study of several fundamental esoteric themes (the Myth of Thule, Agartha, Shambala, etc.) which have come under discussion in connection with National Socialism, by a writer with expert knowledge of esoteric streams and motifs. This book is especially estimable because Godwin deals with these motifs in their European and indeed their world-wide context and within a broad framework of time – chiefly between 1850 and 1950. He thus looks beyond a temporally and spatially narrow (German) perspective.

Nicholas Goodrick-Clarke, *The Occult Roots of Nazism: Secret Aryan Cults and their Influence on Nazi Ideology*, Tauris Parke 2012

A fundamentally (indeed the) historically and philologically detailed investigation into the esoteric 'ariosophic' groups around the ambit of rising National Socialism. The book tends rather to negate or lack appreciation of the influence of all those groups while also downplaying the subject matter altogether. Goodrick-Clarke's comprehension of esotericism, its content and streams is weak, and this restricts the value of what he has to say.

Eduard Gugenberger, *Hitlers Visionäre – die okkulten Wegbereiter des Dritten Reiches* ('Hitler's visionaries – the occult trailblazers of the Third Reich'), Vienna 2001 (208pp)

Portraits of 'occult trailblazers' of the Third Reich (Schüler, Eckart, Guido von List, Lanz von Liebenfels, Sebottendorf, Wiligut, Otto Rahn, Hanussen, Mathilde Ludendorff, Evola). Written by an anti-esotericist who appears to regard esotericism and National Socialism as two sides of the same coin. From this angle the book is tub-thumping, but otherwise it is thoroughly researched and interesting.

Karl Heyer, *Wesen und Wollen des Nationalsozialismus* ('The nature and intent of National Socialism'), 3rd Edition, Basel 1991. Initially in 1947: *Wenn die Götter den Tempel verlassen* ('When the Gods Abandon the Temple'); then, in 1965: *Der Staat als Werkzeug des Bösen* ('The state as a tool of evil'), (438 pp), out of print, new edition planned.

An admirable work on National Socialism, focussing on the various aspects as phenomena. Not sensationalist, and yet incisive. Written from the angle of a contemporary who in some instances forms his very wide perspective on the basis of seemingly insignificant every-day details. Heyer (1888–1967) was perhaps the most important anthroposophical historian of the generation following Rudolf Steiner.

Ellic Howe, *Urania's Children: The Strange World of the Astrologers*, Kimber 1967

An investigation firstly into the survival, or re-emergence, of astrology in modern Europe, and then of Karl Ernst Krafft, who played a role in the Third Reich. The book arose out of decades of engagement with the subject matter. During World War II the author (1910–1991) was a member of the British SOE (Special Operations Executive) which also concerned itself with the utilization of astrology. He was a Freemason and an outstanding authority on the 'occult underground' from the nineteenth to the twentieth century.

Christoph Lindenberg, *Die Technik des Bösen – zur Geschichte und Vorgeschichte des Nationalsozialismus* ('The technique of evil – on the history and pre-history of National Socialism'), 3rd edition, Stuttgart 1985 (initially 1977, 110 pp.)

A response – although not described as such – to Tautz by a historian, pedagogue and anthroposophist. The book has a tendency to downplay all occult connections and consider them unimportant. There appears to be a background idea that emphasizing the occult power of National Socialism amounts to downplaying the moral responsibilities of those who supported it.

Peter Orzechowski, *Braune Macht und Schwarze Magie* ('Brown power and black magic'), Ravensburg, no date (around 1982, 239 pp., out of print)

An interesting investigation of both the sources and the possible origins of the magical and esoteric elements of National Socialism, and of the way they manifested, for instance in the matters of Hitler's rhetoric and the techniques of mass suggestion and mass manipulation.

Trevor Ravenscroft, *Spear of Destiny: The Occult Power behind the Spear which Pierced the Side of Christ*, Red Wheel/Weiser, 2nd Edition 1983

A gripping book which initially sets out to depict the significance of the Holy Spear in relation to the thinking of the Third Reich. It then proceeds to present developments in Germany during the early decades of the twentieth century as a battle between the black magicians around Hitler and the white magicians around Rudolf Steiner and Walter Johannes Stein. Regrettably, truth and phantasy (perhaps even lies) are so bewilderingly intertwined in this book that one is obliged to regard it as fiction and not fit for purpose.

Michael Rissmann, *Hitlers Gott — Vorsehungsglaube und Sendungsbe-wusstsein des deutschen Diktators* ('Hitler's god — The belief in destiny and sense of mission of the German dictator'), Zurich/Munich, 2001, (313pp)

Rissmann endeavours to interpret Hitler's idea of God on the basis of literature, in order to fathom which religion was really at work in the Third Reich and where it came from. He worked his way through an almost unimaginable amount of literature. Some of the literary criticism is valuable, but on the whole the book suffers from ideas about things such as 'religion', 'world view', or 'influence' that are too wooden, and there is a lack of imaginative quality in dealing with the sources.

Detlev Rose, *Die Thule-Gesellschaft — Legende, Mythos, Wirklichkeit* ('The Thule Society — legend, myth, reality'), Tübingen, 1994 (271pp)

A historically and philologically sound work on the Thule Society as it appeared in Munich at the end of World War I. However, it lacks any profound understanding of the occult streams and connections and is therefore inadequate in this field.

Rüdiger Sünner, *Schwarze Sonne — Entfesselung und Missbrauch der Mythen in Nationalsozialismus und rechter Esoteric* ('Black sun — the unleashing and misuse of myths in National Socialism and right-wing esotericism'), 2nd edition, Freiburg i.Br. 1999 (256pp)

A depiction of myths and esoteric motifs as they occurred in National Social-ism, forming the beliefs and rites of the SS. (Pleasing in that the author does not condemn esotericism out of hand.)

Notes

Chapter 1

1. Emil Bock, 'Vom Mythos des Nationalsozialismus', in *Die Christengemeinschaft*, 1948, p. 34 ff.
2. Hans Mommsen, 'Der Reichstagsbrand und seine politischen Folgen', supplement from *Das Parlament*, 11 November 1964.
3. Hermann Rauschning, *The Voice of Destruction*, G.P. Putnam, New York 1940. A former Nazi politician, Rauschning broke away from Nazism before the Second World War.
4. André François-Poncet (1887–1978), French politician and diplomat. He wrote several books based on his experiences as the French Ambassador to Germany between 1931 and 1938.
5. Folkert Wilken (1890–1981), *Geistesgeschichtliche Entwicklungslinien des deutschen Schicksals*, Stuttgart 1948. Wilken was an anthroposophist and, from 1925, a professor of economics at the University of Freiburg.
6. See 'Rückschau nach dreissig Jahren. Hitlers Machtergreifung in der Sicht deutscher und ausländischer Historiker' supplement from *Das Parlament*, 30 January 1963.
7. *Obrigkeit*: authority. *Frommheit*: piety. Obedience to the ruler as act of piety.
8. Alfred Rosenberg, *Der Mythos des zwanzigsten Jahrhunderts* (1930). A bestseller in Germany, it has been published in English as *The Myth of the Twentieth Century*. Rosenberg was one of the main authors of Nazi ideology, including its racial theory leading to extreme anti-Semitism and Hitler's genocidal policies. The 'Myth' in the title refers to the ideal of pure Aryan blood, the Nordics being the 'master race' superior to all others, and to the awakening of the 'racial soul'.
9. Karl Jaspers, *Wohin treibt die Bundesrepublik?*, Piper, 1966. Translated as *The Future of Germany*, University of Chicago Press 1967.
10. Emil Bock, *The Apocalypse of Saint John*, Christian Community Press 1957.
11. Karl Löwith (1897–1973), German philosopher and prolific writer.
12. Rudolf Steiner, lecture of 14 August 1924, in *True and False Paths* (CW 243), Rudolf Steiner Press 1985.

13. Eduard Mörike (1805–85), one of Germany's greatest Romantic poets.
14. Rudolf Steiner, lectures of 28 & 29 December 1923, in *World History in the Light of Anthroposophy* (CW 233), Rudolf Steiner Press 1977.

Chapter 2

1. See Rudolf Steiner, *From Beetroot to Buddhism* (CW 353), Rudolf Steiner Press 1999.
2. Emil Leinhas, *Aus der Arbeit mit Rudolf Steiner*, Basel 1950.
3. Hannah Arendt (1906–75), German-American political theorist and philosopher, author of *The Origins of Totalitarianism*, Schocken Books 1951.
4. *The Fall of the Spirits of Darkness* (CW 178), Rudolf Steiner Press 1993.
5. Rudolf Steiner, *From Beetroot to Buddhism* (CW 353), Rudolf Steiner Press 1999.
6. Dalai Lama, *My Land and My People*, 1962. His second autobiography, *Freedom in Exile*, was published in 1989.
7. Arthur de Gobineau (1816–82) became famous for developing the theory of the Aryan master race in his book *An Essay on the Inequality of Races* (1853–5). It was republished under the title *The Inequality of Human Races* in 1915 by G.P. Putnam's Sons (London) and Heinemann (NY).
8. See Rudolf Steiner, *The Archangel Michael, His Mission and Ours*, Lecture of 29 November 1919, SteinerBooks 1994.
9. Rainer Hildebrandt, *Wir sind die Letzten*, Neuwied-Berlin 1933.

Chapter 3

1. Rudolf Steiner, lecture of 29 November 1919 in *The Archangel Michael*, SteinerBooks 1994.
2. Wilhelm Bitter (Ed.), *Massenwahn in Geschichte und Gegenwart*, Stuttgart 1965.
3. C. G. Jung, *Aufsätze zur Zeitgeschichte*, Zurich 1946.
4. Alfred Weber, *Der dritte oder der vierte Mensch, Vom Sinn des menschlichen Daseins*, Munich 1953.
5. See Paul Arnsberg, Wolfgang Scheffler: 'Zu Hannah Arendts "Eichmann in Jerusalem"', in supplement of *Das Parlament*, 4 November 1964.
6. Lectures of 11, 12 and 13 October 1918.

7. Karl Heyer, *Wenn die Götter den Tempel verlassen* ('When the Gods Abandon the Temple'), 1947.

8. Rudolf Steiner, 18 September 1924, *Karmic Relationships* Vol. IV (GA 238), Rudolf Steiner Press 1997.

9. See Rudolf Meyer, *Der Gral und seine Hüter* ('The Grail and its Guardians'), Stuttgart 1956.

10. Friedrich Häusler, 'Aus den sizilianischen Rätseln', in *Das Goetheanum*, 24 October 1937. Also 'Klingsor', *Das Goetheanum*, 8 May 1938.

11. Ernst Uehli, *Die drei grossen Staufer*, Dornach 1961. See also Harry Köhler, 'Von der Königin Sibilia von Sizilien und dem Herzoge von Terra de Labur', in *Das Goetheanum*, 31 May 1931.

12. See Alfred Schütze: 'Die Menschheit an der Schwelle der geistigen Welt' in *Die Christengemeinschaft*, 1957, p. 230..

13. Rudolf Steiner: lecture of 6 February 1913, in *The Mysteries of the East and of Christianity* (CW 144), Rudolf Steiner Press 1972.

14. See Alfred Schütze, *The Enigma of Evil*, Floris Books, Edinburgh 1978.

15. Herbert Hahn, *Christus in der ätherischen Welt*, Zeist 1963.

16. Karl König, 'Geschichte und Schicksal des jüdischen Volkes', private manuscript.

Appendix

1. The *Flensburger Hefte* have already undertaken some research into the relationship between Anthroposophy and National Socialism, which also dealt with earlier articles of the *Völkische Beobachter* ('Anthroposophists and National Socialism', No.31/1991).

2. See also: Jacob Ruchti/Helmuth von Moltke, *Der Ausbruch des Ersten Weltkrieges – zwei vergessene zentrale Schriften zum Verständnis der Vorgänge bei Kriegsausbruch 1914 und der Haltung Rudolf Steiners* (published with an introduction by Andreas Bracher, Basel 2001). ('The outbreak of World War I—two forgotten articles on an understanding of events in 1914 and Rudolf Steiner's point of view')

3. 'Ein eigentümlicher Theosoph' ('A peculiar theosophist') in: *Auf gut Deutsch*, 11.7.1919, pp.322–327, and 'Der Adler des Jupiter' ('The eagle of Jupiter') in: *Auf gut Deutsch*, 12.12.1919, pp.659–672. Markus Osterieder, Munich, drew my attention to these two articles.

4. There are some interesting remarks about his experiences in *völkisch* circles in Heise's book, written in 1923, *Der katholische Ansturm wider den Okkultismus und sein tiefgreifender Einfluss auf das allgemeine Völkerleben* ('The Catholic attack against occultism and its profound influence on the general life of nations'), reprinted by Cagliostro Verlag, Rotterdam, no date.

5. *Soziales Verständnis aus geisteswissenschaftlicher Erkenntnis*, CW 191, lecture of 3.10.1919 (not translated). It is not entirely clear what is meant by 'Central Europe' in this case—whether the usual Germany together with the Western Slav region is meant, or Germany alone. Central Europe is here mentioned in contradistinction to Switzerland, which might therefore be construed as referring specifically to Germany.